ROBERT LOWELL'S POEMS
A Selection

also by Robert Lowell

Robert Lowell's Poems

A SELECTION

edited with
an introduction and notes
by
JONATHAN RABAN

FABER AND FABER
3 Queen Square
London

First published in 1974
by Faber and Faber Limited
3 Queen Square London WC1
Printed in Great Britain by
Latimer Trend & Company Ltd Plymouth
All rights reserved

ISBN 0 571 10182 8
(paper covers)

ISBN 0 571 10594 7
(hard bound edition)

Contents

from *For the Union Dead*

from *Near the Ocean*

from *Notebook*

(These poems are printed in the order in which they orginally appeared in the 1970 edition of *Notebook*; their texts are taken from *History* and *For Lizzie and Harriet*.)

from *The Dolphin*

Introduction

The poetry of Robert Lowell is as difficult, and as exciting, as any that has been written in our time. It is a proud, private, hugely ambitious body of work, and it makes no obvious concessions to its readers. Lowell challenges one to be as intelligent, as imaginatively quick, and as well-read as he is himself, and the challenge is one that few readers will be able to take up with any confidence. When Lowell writes about the twentieth century, he is likely to take us there via seventeenth-century poetry, mediaeval theology, ancient history and classical philosophy. To fix the present moment, he is prepared to range up against it all that he knows of what has been thought and done and written in the past. Yet his poems are instinct with contemporaneity; they tell us more of what it means to live, painfully and difficultly, in our century than any writer has previously dared. For Lowell has not shirked confrontation with the darkest and most personal of his own experiences: a term in jail, spells in mental hospital, marriages, loss of faith ... he has lived as fully in the world as any writer can, and his poems report, with great honesty and intelligence, from that battlefield. As he said to Stanley Kunitz, 'It may be that some people have turned to my poems because of the very things that are wrong with me, I mean the difficulty I have with ordinary living, the impracticability, the myopia.' His vision is powerful and long-ranging, but it takes into account the ordinary failure, the flights of depression and disillusion, the puzzlement and the unhappiness of most of our lives most of the time. His poetry is written with a humility that makes it, for all its references and allusions, available—and perhaps necessary—to us all. His contemporary, Elizabeth Bishop, has said of him: 'Somehow or other, by fair means or foul, and in the middle of our worst century so far, we have produced a magnificent poet.'

Lowell himself was convinced of his own vocation. From early in his life he dedicated himself to his writing with passionate and total seriousness. He was born in 1917, into an old and powerful Boston family. There is a famous folk rhyme about Boston—

> *Home of the bean and the cod*
> *Where the Lowells talk only to Cabots*
> *And the Cabots talk only to God.*

Boston's second family included the nineteenth-century American poet James Russell Lowell and the experimental poet of the 1910s and 20s, Amy Lowell. Lowell has said of Amy that she was 'big and a scandal, as if Mae West were a cousin'. He went on: 'My immediate family, if you have an English equivalent, would be the Duke of Something's sixth cousins. We gave no feeling of swagger.' He was an only child, and his descriptions of his boyhood, in the poems in *Life Studies*, and in the superb prose piece, '91 Revere Street', are spiky with recollected shyness and tension—his 'fogbound solitudes' as he calls them in 'Dunbarton'. To be born a Bostonian was to inherit a fading tradition. From the seventeenth to the nineteenth century the great families of New England had been the spiritual and cultural leaders of America. From Boston and its environs came the Puritan divines—Increase and Cotton Mather, Jonathan Edwards, Edward Taylor—and America's foremost nineteenth-century writers—Emerson, Thoreau, Melville, Hawthorne. But by the twentieth century this tradition of excellence had become little more than a memory. Lowell's own family were shabby gentry: they attended church, but as unbelievers. 'Faith was improper,' Lowell has said of them: faith, the cornerstone of New England's past, had turned, by Lowell's boyhood, into an object of mild social embarrassment. It was proper, the traditional thing, for a Boston aristocrat to go to Harvard, and Lowell matriculated there. But he was unhappy and unsuccessful as a Harvard student, and at the end of his first year, he changed colleges and went to Kenyon University in Ohio, to study under John Crowe Ransom. It was an ideal move for a young writer. Lowell left the genteel remnants of one tradition for the confident renaissance of another. At Kenyon, the New Criticism was gathering vitality: the essays and poems of Ransom, Tate, Randall Jarrell, Yvor Winters and R. P. Blackmur were full of just the kind of imaginative verve and assurance that was so lacking in Lowell's native New England. The South had been defeated in the American Civil War, and by the 1930s, Southern writers were vigorously defining a new, purged Southern identity. Lowell came to Kenyon a pilgriming yankee ready to learn from the Southerner. He pitched a tent in the Tates' back garden, took dictation from Ford Madox Ford who was staying as a guest in the Tates' house, and plunged himself into an energetic reading of the classics. In a recent interview, Lowell has said:

> Tate and Ransom, poets and critics, were Southerners and the line they took was that Southerners looked at the whole thing, and not just at intellect like a Yankee. If Ransom writes a poem about a man and a woman, the man is Calvinist and the woman a Southerner who knows flowers, the flesh, beauty and children. One might say that Catholicism notices things, the particular, while Calvinism studies the attenuate ideal. I have been too deep in that dogfight ever to get out.

Lowell became a Catholic convert in 1940, the year of his graduation from Kenyon, and the year of his marriage, to Jean Stafford, the Colorado novelist. It was as much a conversion to a style of sensibility, a way of thinking and feeling, as it was a conversion to a particular religious practice. As a Catholic, Lowell was dramatically able to reject the narrow intellection of New England. Later, he was to lose the faith he had won at the age of twenty-three. He said recently: 'I don't believe, but I am a sort of gospeller, I like to read Christ's own words.'

His early poems (those selected in this edition from *Poems 1938–1949*) are absorbed in the twin problem of religion and literary tradition. Can the order of faith, or the order of metre, metaphor, rhyme, strict form, still work in a century whose contact with its historical roots grows ever more shaky? Lowell, with his education in Classics, as recommended by Tate, his ear for and grounding in seventeenth-century verse, his fresh, sensual Catholicism, holds his traditions to the modern world and waits to see which will burn first. There is a constant sense of abrasion, of incongruity, of the tug and turmoil of a man whose head is full of history but whose eyes can only pick out the contemporary urban sprawl of used-car lots and utility housing projects, and the spiritual and technological junk of the Second World War. In a *Paris Review* interview given in 1960, Lowell said of both his and Allen Tate's writing, 'We wanted our formal patterns to seem a hardship and something we couldn't rattle off easily.' It's a characteristic understatement. The language of these early poems bulges and splits with the effort of containment; the vocabulary is clotted, syntax and metre buckle under the pressure of experience. Sometimes it seems enough for a poem to be a simple catalogue of dissonances, ancient and modern flung against each other to see if some revealing symbol can be squeezed out from their odd union. The first nine lines of a sonnet called 'Concord', for instance:

> *Ten thousand Fords are idle here in search*
> *Of a tradition. Over these dry sticks—*
> *The Minute Man, the Irish Catholics,*
> *The ruined bridge and Walden's fished-out perch—*
> *The belfry of the Unitarian Church*
> *Rings out the hanging Jesus. Crucifix,*
> *How can your whited spindling arms transfix*

> *Mammon's unbridled industry, the lurch*
> *For forms to harness Heraclitus' stream!*

Concord was the village centre of nineteenth-century American Transcendentalism. There Thoreau built his hut on the bank of Walden pond, and Emerson produced his strings of immaculate epigrams. Concord embodies the proudest and most mandarin aspects of New England's religious and philosophical traditions. But in Lowell's poem it has deteriorated into a catalogue of fruitless discords. It was, indeed, Heraclitus, the philosopher of flux, who remarked that no harmony could exist without discord, but Heraclitus had not set eyes upon the urban jungle of twentieth-century America. In this stew of fecund industry and exhausted nature, the crucifix has an impossible job to do. Notice, incidentally, how, although the sentence has the form of a question, it finishes with an exclamation mark—an expression of astonished, embattled resignation before the sheer promiscuity of experience.

'Lowell,' said R. P. Blackmur, 'is distraught about religion.' And Gabriel Pearson expanded the point in a memorable and accurate phrase in his discussion of 'In Memory of Arthur Winslow': 'It is with a kind of hysterical giggle that Lowell launches his Jesus upon the waters.' When Lowell's Christianity comes up against the modern world, the collision is never far from entailing a rueful, bizarre comedy. In 'The Holy Innocents', for instance, watch how Lowell drives the oxen of Bethlehem towards the chromium automobiles of Christmas 1945. His nativity scene is a monstrous hybrid; his holy infant might have been painted by Francis Bacon, a Buchenwald Jesus, without dignity or divinity:

> *King Herod shrieking vengeance at the curled*
> *Up knees of Jesus choking in the air,*

Yet the second stanza of the poem moves to a seemingly unachievable placidity and tenderness, a triumph of grace over circumstances:

> *If they die,*
> *As Jesus, in the harness, who will mourn?*
> *Lamb of the shepherds, Child, how still you lie.*

It is easy to label these last-line reversals, these sudden retrievals of faith or tradition, as 'reconciliations', but they reconcile little or nothing. We are presented with, on the one hand, a kind of aborted possibility, a twisted wreck of what-might-have-been, and on the other, a triumphant celebration of a spiritual life that continues against all the odds. Both are there in the poem, and neither, finally, will budge. Experience is implacably dualistic, and though it can acquire poetic shape and direction it can never escape from paradox. Many of the early poems seem simply concerned to talk experience out; an act undertaken, perhaps, in desperation, but carried through with a steely joy in the process of turning life to symbol, metaphor, the pulse of metre and the magical recurrence of rhyme.

There's something strangely cheerful about the way Lowell dons his robes as a lord of misrule. His habitual five-beat line is jaunty, a rhythm to jog along in at a great pace, riding over the contradictions and brute paradoxes which it encounters on the way.

> *Is there no way to cast my hook*
> *Out of this dynamited brook?*

—he demands, in 'The Drunken Fisherman', and though the words are framed in anguish, they are sprung in the line with a kind of manic zest. There is, too, a tremendous associative freedom of language, a shorthand of images that boil and burst from one another, as if Lowell had been able to plug into the high-voltage circuitry of the Elizabethan and Jacobean dramatists. He frequently rises to an English of crackling, Renaissance splendour. Try following this self-generating cascade of metaphor from 'Between the Porch and the Altar':

> *Time runs, the windshield runs with stars. The past*

Is cities from a train, until at last
Its escalating and black-windowed blocks
Recoil against a Gothic church. The clocks
Are tolling. I am dying. The shocked stones
Are falling like a ton of bricks and bones
That snap and splinter and descend in glass
Before a priest who mumbles through his Mass
And sprinkles holy water; and the Day
Breaks with its lightning on the man of clay,

In the poem we are asked to imagine these words as the mono-
logue of a drunken man sitting in a nightclub with his girl,
watching a floor show of ice-skaters. But drunkenness, or
mania, in Lowell's verse, works as a dramatic convention; it
licenses a linguistic flood of images, associations, visionary
experiences which escape the hard-boiled syntax of ordinary
rationality. So here a whole complex of themes are densely
woven together: time passes, with clocks that 'toll' rather than
'tick', towards a daybreak that is both a real dawn and the
lightning-flash of Armageddon; and the movement of time is
made concrete by the travelling motor car and train; simultane-
ously, we're made to see the historical confrontation between
the secular city with its office blocks and skyscrapers and the
religious city with its church and celebrating priest; in the
process, what sounds like the bomb damage of a blitz turns out,
mysteriously, to be that capitalized Day when God's wrath
breaks over His creation. As in a dream or an alcoholic daze,
there's no clear distinction between 'real' and 'imagined' ex-
perience; all is metaphor, violent, fluid, and elusive. It's a
tremendously powerful passage, and it invites comparisons with
the most metaphorically inventive seventeenth-century verse.
It may help to put Lowell's work in perspective to read this
alongside a rather similar piece by John Donne, from his
verse letter, 'The Storme'. Both work in rhymed iambic
couplets; both push a literal, dramatic experience to the point

where it becomes a ringing theological metaphor. Watch, especially, for the way in which Donne's images, like Lowell's, take over the reins of the poetry, transferring us from the actual situation of a man in a real storm at sea to a poetry of total statement which has to do as much with Man as with 'a man', and with the turmoil of a sinful Creation on the dawn of yet another imagined Armageddon.

> Jonas, *I pitty thee, and curse those men,*
> *Who when the storm rag'd most, did wake thee then;*
> *Sleepe is paines easiest salve, and doth fulfill*
> *All offices of death, except to kill.*
> *But when I wakt, I saw, that I saw not;*
> *Ay, and the Sunne, which should teach mee' had forgot*
> *East, West, Day, Night, and I could onely say,*
> *If 'the world had lasted, now it had been day.*
> *Thousands our noyses were, yet wee' mongst all*
> *Could none by his right name, but thunder call:*
> *Lightning was all our light, and it rain'd more*
> *Than if the Sunne had drunke the sea before.*
> *Some coffin'd in their cabbin lye, 'equally*
> *Griev'd that they are not dead, and yet must dye;*
> *And as sin-burd'ned soules from graves will creepe,*
> *At the last day, some forth their cabbins peepe:*
> *And tremblingly 'aske what newes, and doe heare so,*
> *Like jealous husbands, what they would not know.*

But the society of twentieth-century America, unlike that of seventeenth-century England, has not on the whole been hospitable to such passionate metaphysical styles. While we need to see Lowell's intimate relationship with the tradition of Donne and Marvell, we must also recognize that it is a relationship that survives in an atmosphere of strain and recrimination. As he says, his formal patterns 'seem a hardship', and in order to make them work with the splendid ease of the sequence from 'Between the Porch and the Altar', he needs to put them in the mouth of a drunk. The bottle and the mental hospital figure in his work both as desperately real components of his own life, to be known and countered, and as essential symbols of the estrangement of the modern writer from his tradition. Only in the rhetoric of the mad and the inebriated can the old freedoms and continuities survive. And Lowell has, in his life as well as his writing, kept on the bitter margin of a society and a century with whom he has a lover's profound quarrel. He was imprisoned as a conscientious objector during the Second World War; he made a famous stand against the White House policy on Vietnam during the 1960s; he now lives, not among his 'Furies' in America, but in a green English exile.

The longest and most complicated of Lowell's early poems, like 'The Quaker Graveyard in Nantucket' and 'At the Indian Killer's Grave', are an agonised whirl of tradition and modernity; the voice at their centre is that of a tightrope walker negotiating an abyss bounded on the one hand by a mass-produced secularism, and on the other by a glowing history of religious faith and a confident literary humanism. Watch how, in 'The Quaker Graveyard', Lowell ranges his artillery of classical mythology, the New England whaling tradition, Melville's *Moby Dick*, the figure of Jonah as a surrogate Christ ('Jonas Messias'), and a thickened, neo-Jacobean language, and brings them to bear, in a mourning salute, on his cousin, killed in the North Atlantic in the Second World War. We listen as much to the sheer *difficulty* of measuring up these grand traditional styles and references against the bleak bloodiness of a life lost in a modern war, as to their unquestionable resonance and splendour of effect. Lowell's habitual style is, in his own phrase, 'gristly'. His gifts as a rhetorician are always tempered by a basic honesty of tone which compels him to expose the ash and cinders in the midst of the fine roll and blaze of the poetic line. Yet, never far off, even in the most gristly of his poems, is a vision of triumphant lucidity, an Edenic state where metre comes trippingly to hand, where rhymes fall in perfect cadence and experience can be hooked and caught with the precision and grace of a fly-fisher landing a trout—an image which haunts Lowell's work. But those poems which actually achieve this condition of immaculate lucidity tend to be monologues by figures who are so marginal or maimed that they have effectively taken leave of the reality of society. One of the poems published in *Life Studies*, but in the prefatory section before the famous portraits of his family, is the brilliantly free-floating, ringingly-rhymed speech, 'A Mad Negro Soldier Confined At Munich'. The white aristocratic pacifist has only society's margin to share with a black G.I.—the final democracy of mania.

> *Cat-houses talk cold turkey to my guards;*
> *I found my* fraulein *stitching outing shirts*
> *in the black forest of the colored wards—*
> *lieutenants squawked like chickens in her skirts.*
>
> *Her German language made my arteries harden—*
> *I've no annuity from the pay we blew.*
> *I chartered an aluminum canoe,*
> *I had her six times in the English Garden.*

The syntax of the verse has an egotistical dislocation; it creates a first-person universe where *I* is the centre and sole cause. The clear finality of every statement is both the price and the prize of madness; and only in madness can such images of surreal exactitude be framed. 'A Mad Negro Soldier' is a distillation of both the strongest features of Lowell's poetry and everything that it is not. Like Lowell, the mad negro speaks from the void of isolation, in a frenetic rhetoric of glittering phrases; unlike Lowell, he has succeeded in dissolving the outside world altogether, until he and his fellow prisoners have become like the fish in a tank—

> *. . . fancy minnows, slaves of habit, shoot*
> *like starlight through their air-conditioned bowl.*

For Lowell, no such dissolution, or mad objectivity, is possible —though its distant presence is constantly being hinted at. The tragic predicament of the negro soldier and the tragic force of his writing are opposites in kind, though mutually complementary. The world is there to be reckoned with, not moved away like a stone in front of a cave, or a tomb.

The biographical poems in *Life Studies* are just such an extended reckoning with the world. Their rhythms are provisional and tetchy; rhymes come to them only occasionally, seemingly by accident. Indeed some critics, notably Ian Hamilton in an essay in *The Review*, have said that Lowell's writing in poems like 'Commander Lowell' is so flat and prosy that it is hardly poetry at all. Certainly he had relinquished the driving rhetoric and rhythm of the English Metaphysicals for a language that was closer in tone to the irregular, 'talky' metre of William Carlos Williams. But quite unlike Williams's affectionate portraits of the patients in his doctor's practice, Lowell's family album is mounted in anguish, phrased in desperation. John Bayley catches the flavour of this new direction in Lowell's work in a brilliant critical comment: 'The words of the early poems lie about helplessly, turgid and swollen: the words of the later ones achieve a crispness of cancellation, leaving behind them only a kind of acrid exhaust smell.'

The title of the collection smacked of the academy and its formal exercises. In his early work, Lowell had shown his immensely resourceful verbal inventiveness and his genius for pastiche. Now he seems to have abandoned, cancelled out, all the bold rhetorical effects; he had put the consolations of literary tradition in temporary abeyance, and had come to his own life and family like a lone mountaineer, testing what bare minimum of equipment was necessary for the climb. Or, to take up the metaphor in the title, he had returned to the basic economy of line drawing and pure draughtsmanship, without benefit of the dramatic force and opportunities for patching-up and concealment afforded by paint. His poems 'from the life' have a deliberate severity of technique; and Lowell makes as few concessions as he can to either the wealth or the evasive craft of the rhetorician in himself. From 'My Last Afternoon With Uncle Devereux Winslow':

> *While I sat on the tiles,*
> *and dug at the anchor on my sailor blouse,*
> *Uncle Devereux stood behind me.*
> *He was as brushed as Bayard, our riding horse.*
> *His face was putty.*
> *His blue coat and white trousers*
> *grew sharper and straighter.*
> *His coat was a blue jay's tail,*
> *his trousers were solid cream from the top of the bottle.*
> *He was animated, hierarchical,*
> *like a ginger snap man in a clothes-press.*
> *He was dying of the incurable Hodgkin's disease. . . .*
> *My hands were warm, then cool, on the piles*
> *of earth and lime,*
> *a black pile and a white pile. . . .*
> *Come winter,*
> *Uncle Devereux would blend to the one colour.*

The possibilities of metaphor and simile have been narrowed down from the brimming treasure trove of Lowell's earlier verse to the domestic horizons of the child. The family horse, putty, the blue jay, the ginger-snap man, the piles of earth and lime, have taken the place of the rag-bag of literary and religious allusions; Lowell has drastically reduced the range of his palette, and his effects here have to rely on the delicate and the exact rather than the bold and the instantly striking. Gone, too, is the galloping, catch-as-catch-can metre. Each line orchestrates either one, or two, or three two-beat phrases that chime with the /ᵛ/ᵛᵛ pattern of 'Uncle Devereux'. Though the poem is, in fact, rhymed, we notice only the nagging, ragged echoes of one word on another, for Lowell is working with uneasy half-rhymes that sound surreptitiously through the flat syntax of the poem. The same tentativeness afflicts the sparks of association that are struck in the verse. Uncle Devereux's cream trousers are the same colour as the milk on the top of the bottle, and the phrase seems fleetingly, to suggest the notion of aristocracy, the social 'cream' from, vulgarly, 'the top drawer'. It's an association which is strengthened by the use of the word 'hierarchical' in the next line, but Lowell leaves it as a troubling hint of the New England gentility that is dying with Uncle Devereux in his immaculate trousers. And there is that line, 'He was dying of the incurable Hodgkin's disease', which seems to lie out of the range of poetry altogether; a statement of fact which eludes even the vaguest and most inclusive of the metrical shapes which bind the verse, and which half-rhymes, irritatingly and with the kind of bizarre appositeness which might occur by chance to a child but be quite inexplicable, with 'clothes-press'. The tremulous, unfocused character of the verse awaits its resolution in the last line. Suddenly Lowell springs on us, from the barest of raw materials, a resounding metaphor. The monotone of death becomes the greyness into which all history, all tradition, must inexorably sink. All the loosenesses, the dispossessed details, the faint hints, of the rest of the poem settle into a firm order behind the last line. We discover in retrospect that what Lowell was doing was keeping all the ingredients of the poem in a state of fluid suspension, floating in readiness for the net with which, in a single movement, he could scoop them up and contain them. Lowell frequently invests the final lines of his poems with this kind of responsibility for total command; sometimes, as here, they measure up magnificently to the job.

The poems in *Life Studies* all negotiate with experience very close-in; they move complicatedly and with great and careful calculation, and we shouldn't mistake their determined avoidance of large scale, seventeenth-century strategies for mere prosy chattiness. On the contrary, they make much of Lowell's earlier work look, by comparison, like florid pastiche. But, more than any other collection by Lowell, *Life Studies* has been widely and wilfully misread. Because these poems deal with the poet's private family and (notably in 'Waking In The Blue' and 'Home After Three Months Away') his experience in a mental hospital, they were quickly and casually labelled as 'confessional verse'—a label which took fire and has since been used to yoke Lowell together with such ill-chosen accomplices as Sylvia Plath and Anne Sexton—both of whom have been influenced by Lowell's writing but with whom he actually shares very little. Gabriel Pearson gave a spirited rebuttal to this view of Lowell: 'In explicitly treating his life as materials, he was not making his poetry more personal but depersonalizing his own life.' Every careful reader of *Life Studies* and the volumes that have followed it must endorse Pearson's statement, for the notion that the book is a kind of locked trunk of confessions, gossip and scandal has, for far too long, got in the way of a serious consideration of its most important triumphs—triumphs of artifice, of artistic distance and control, of fashioning a language that will correspond to the centrality, in a century of mass culture, of man as a private person. In *Life Studies*, Lowell used his own family, his own life, like pieces of litmus paper; he watched them colouring under the acid of contemporary history. In his earlier work it had been his faith and his literary tradition that had been exposed in this way; now it was the turn of the self, at its most intimate and vulnerable. When, in 'Waking in the Blue', Lowell writes:

> *Cock of the walk,*
> *I strut in my turtle-necked French sailor's jersey*
> *before the metal shaving mirrors,*
> *and see the shaky future grow familiar*
> *in the pinched, indigenous faces*
> *of these thoroughbred mental cases,*
> *twice my age and half my weight.*

We are all old-timers,
each of us holds a locked razor.

—the personal experience of the poem has become reborn as metaphor. Who are 'we'? At the most literal level, the 'thoroughbred mental cases' are all rich New Englanders, the pathetically raddled products of Ivy League universities and their prestigious fraternities. The 'old-timers' have a long sentence of history and tradition behind them; and perhaps it is really the exhausted tradition of New England itself that is twice Lowell's age and half his weight. And the possibilities of individual action have been drastically cut down; the razors are locked, the mirrors made of unbreakable metal. It is at once a poem about a man in a mental hospital and a grim portrait of Man surviving amongst the relics of his history. This readiness to use his own experience as a pulse on which to sound the state of the body politic has been a steady feature of Lowell's later poetry. Randall Jarrell once described Lowell's mind as 'anthropomorphic', and it's a useful word. For he is, in his poems, as much *anthropos* as Lowell; a figure of representative man through whom human experience at large may be encountered and understood. He has humbled himself before history; and that act, of the imaginative sacrifice of the self, has given his work its greatest dignity.

Life Studies was a purgation; in that collection he pared his poetry down to a line of necessity. Since *Life Studies* his work has been able to reabsorb the rhetorical power and rich allusiveness of his early verse, but he has kept them tempered by a constant and severe awareness of the imminence of the temporary, the provisional, the mortality of the poetic line amid the flux and danger of twentieth-century life. Of his next collection, *For the Union Dead*, Lowell has said:

Depression's no gift from the Muse. At worst, I do nothing. But often I've written, and wrote one whole book—*For the Union Dead*—about witheredness. It wasn't acute depression,

27

and I felt quite able to work for hours, write and rewrite. Most of the best poems, the most personal, are gathered crumbs. I had better moods, but the book is lemony, soured and dry, the drouth I had touched with my own hands. That too may be poetry—on sufferance.

And the last stanza of 'Eye and Tooth' might stand as an epigraph for the whole collection:

> *Nothing! No oil*
> *for the eye, nothing to pour*
> *on those waters or flames.*
> *I am tired. Everyone's tired of my turmoil.*

The rhetoric has loosened up; the metre begins to roll again; metaphor springs more easily in the mind; but it is calculatedly measured against a corresponding disillusion and deadness of the soul. The 'savage servility' that 'slides by on grease' which concludes the title poem is a violent and powerful image for a terrible world that has grown oppressively close; but Lowell now, unlike the Lowell of the early poems, takes little pleasure in being able to retrieve such spoils of metaphor from the world's welter. The poetry of *For the Union Dead* seems to force itself peremptorily upon the poet. When Lowell's first collection appeared, Allen Tate observed that the symbolic language gave the impression of being 'willed'; here it is unwilled, importunate, merely necessary—as if the poet were the victim of external reality's own dreadful prosody.

Yet in 1967, with the publication of *Near the Ocean*, Lowell appeared to have made some sort of final pact with his tradition, especially in the best of all his public poems, 'Waking Early Sunday Morning'. He had borrowed the metre and stanza form from Marvell's 'The Garden', that eloquent seventeenth-century voyage in search of a private Eden:

> *Fair quiet, have I found thee here,*
> *An Innocence thy Sister dear!*

> *Mistaken long, I sought you then*
> *In busie Companies of Men.*
> *Your sacred Plants, if here below,*
> *Only among the Plants will grow*
> *Society is all but rude,*
> *To this delicious Solitude,*

But in Lowell's poem, the solace of solitude and contemplation has to be hastily snatched on Sunday only, from the turmoil of a secular world of corrupt and mismanaged politics—a world which Marvell's divine Gardener had abandoned to the weeds.

> *How well the skilful Gardener drew*
> *Of flow'rs and herbes this Dial new . . .*

said Marvell, and Lowell grimly corrected him, in terms of the New England—that failed Eden—of the mid-1960s:

> *When will we see Him face to face?*
> *Each day, He shines through darker glass—*
> *In this small town where everything*
> *is known, I see His vanishing*
> *emblems, His white spire and flag-*
> *pole sticking out above the fog,*
> *like old white china doorknobs, sad,*
> *slight, useless things to calm the mad.*

There were to be 'no weekends for the gods now', and Lowell celebrated the disturbances in the contemporary garden in a surge of lyrical power, blending a vivid talent for pastiche with a hard, cold, inventive eye for the actualities of his own political situation. 'Waking Early Sunday Morning' is as rich and re-sounding as anything in his early poems, but it has put into practice the lessons of *Life Studies*, the acid virtues of being spare and cunning. It presents us with a poet of the twentieth century holding a fruitful dialogue, on an even footing, with one of his seventeenth-century masters, and it points directly forward to the sonnet sequence that Lowell started work on as soon as *Near the Ocean* was published.

Notebook, Lowell has said, 'is in unrhymed, loose blank verse sonnets, a roomier stanza, less a prosodist's darling. It can say almost anything conversation or correspondence can'. The form allowed him, he went on, 'rhetoric, formal construction, and quick breaks'. In the sixteenth and seventeenth centuries, the sonnet sequence had enshrined a notion of order and control. 'We'll build in sonnets pretty rooms,' said Donne in 'The Canonization'. Lowell's sonnets are rarely pretty; they are like cluttered modern apartments, stacked with mental bric-à-brac, always restrained on the verge of total disorder. Their language is rangy; flat talk gives way to sinuous poetic hyperbole, elaborate metaphysical conceits fade into gossip. The poems in *Notebook* were written fast, and they are rich in both the dross and the gold of the temporary: in chance conversations, marginal notes to books, letters received, night-thoughts, private games. They have what Lowell calls a 'plot', but its shape is seasonal; it revolves on the cyclic moods and resemblances by which a man may try, uncertainly, to give his life the form and direction of fiction. They compose an epic comedy—something between a single long poem, a novel and an autobiography—whose hero is a writer thrashing out his relationship to history, to tradition, to the balance between public and private life, and to the confused intensity of the immediate moment as it is lived and experienced through the poem. Indeed the first subject of *Notebook* is itself; it is haunted by the possibility of life—even a discontinuous, twentieth-century life in a ravaged literary, political and personal climate—becoming a poem. Both the success and the failure of that possibility are equally important components of *Notebook*.

Reviewing the English edition of *Notebook*, P. N. Furbank remarked that reading the poems was like watching someone balance a ping-pong ball on a jet of water. It's an apt metaphor for the combination of dexterity and countered peril which characterizes the book. Sonnet after sonnet seems about to slip into doggerel, then is retrieved by a brilliant, resonant final line. Syntax and metre are pushed as far as they will go; and Lowell's language is pitched on the edge of some nameless, cataclysmic deterioration, about to slip, perhaps into the blunt ungrammar of the policeman in 'The Restoration', 'Would a human beings do this things to these book?' He is endlessly fascinated with what can go in to his poem without destroying it: letters, snatches of conversation, snippets of quotation, find themselves suddenly dignified by the context of a sonnet, at the same time as they indicate the dangerous edge between the formless flux of the external world and the metrical order of verse.

But, though *Notebook* is written out of the whirlpool of flux and temporaneity, Lowell uses the form to retrieve particular experience with unprecedented brilliance and lucidity. He has found a poetic vernacular in which the immediate moment brushes electrically against history, brooding recollection, and literary reference and comparison. The dialogue constant in all his work between tradition and the modern, between regular form and a language infected with the clutter and decay of contemporary society, is maintained in *Notebook* with a new freedom.

Lowell's latest work, *The Dolphin*, is the summit of his achievement so far. It extends the form of the verse-novel which he had begun to explore in *Notebook*, and its 'plot' is a continuous narrative, telling the story of a love affair, re-marriage and the birth of his first son. It is a poem written in exile; and in England Lowell's writing acquires a new tranquillity of tone. We hear the furies of America offstage, in letters and over the telephone; a far-off war, a painful break-up of a long marriage, the growing intimations of age and death. But at the centre of the poem, Lowell works with a cool power, transforming his life into the lasting eloquence of art by the magical paradox which is itself a major theme of his most recent verse. The individual sonnets, rich and tender, full of delicately adventurous tropes, move to a climax around pregnancy and birth. *The Dolphin* is a work of profound and grateful celebration; from the poet who has written more movingly than anyone else in our time of pain and despair, we have a poem of miraculous deep joy. It has, clearly, been won hard against all odds; and *The Dolphin* is not facile or blind to the anguish and destruction from which its life, and its happiness, have grown. Lowell's future work is not to be anticipated, except to say that he is writing now as bravely and as brilliantly as he has ever done before.

A Note on the Text

For this edition Lowell has made minor amendments to the text of two of his early poems, 'At the Indian Killer's Grave' and 'Mr Edwards and the Spider'. He has greatly shortened and revised 'The Quaker Graveyard in Nantucket' and 'The Drunken Fisherman'. Otherwise the text of this edition follows that of the current English editions of his work. Since Lowell often rewrites and reprints earlier poems as new editions of his work appear, it has sometimes been hard to decide on which versions of a particular poem should be printed here. Usually I have preferred the later text, but on occasions, as with 'New York 1962' I have included the early version (from *For the Union Dead*), although the poem has been reworked later (as a sonnet in *Notebook*). Lowell kindly offered me his advice on the selection, and I have tried to follow his choices as far as space has allowed.

J.R.

from
POEMS 1938—1949

The Holy Innocents

Listen, the hay-bells tinkle as the cart
Wavers on rubber tires along the tar
And cindered ice below the burlap mill
And ale-wife run. The oxen drool and start
In wonder at the fenders of a car,
And blunder hugely up St. Peter's hill.
These are the undefiled by woman—their
Sorrow is not the sorrow of this world:
King Herod shrieking vengeance at the curled
Up knees of Jesus choking in the air,

A king of speechless clods and infants. Still
The world out-Herods Herod; and the year,
The nineteen-hundred forty-fifth of grace,
Lumbers with losses up the clinkered hill
Of our purgation; and the oxen near
The worn foundations of their resting-place,
The holy manger where their bed is corn
And holly torn for Christmas. If they die,
As Jesus, in the harness, who will mourn?
Lamb of the shepherds, Child, how still you lie.

Our Lady of Walsingham

There once the penitents took off their shoes
And then walked barefoot the remaining mile;
And the small trees, a stream and hedgerows file
Slowly along the munching English lane,
Like cows to the old shrine, until you lose
Track of your dragging pain.

The stream flows down under the druid tree,
Shiloah's whirlpools gurgle and make glad
The castle of God. Sailor, you were glad
And whistled Sion by that stream. But see:

Our Lady, too small for her canopy,
Sits near the altar. There's no comeliness
At all or charm in that expressionless
Face with its heavy eyelids. As before,
This face, for centuries a memory,
Non est species, neque decor,
Expressionless, expresses God: it goes
Past castled Sion. She knows what God knows,
Not Calvary's Cross nor crib at Bethlehem
Now, and the world shall come to Walsingham.

The Quaker Graveyard in Nantucket
(FOR WARREN WINSLOW, DEAD AT SEA)

Let man have dominion over the fishes of the sea and the fowls of the air and the beasts and the whole earth, and every creeping creature that moveth upon the earth.

I

A brackish reach of shoal off Madaket,—
The sea was still breaking violently and night
Had steamed into our North Atlantic Fleet,
When the drowned sailor clutched the drag-net. Light
Flashed from his matted head and marble feet,
He grappled at the net
With the coiled, hurdling muscles of his thighs:
The corpse was bloodless, a botch of reds and whites,
Its open, staring eyes

Were lustreless dead-lights
Or cabin-windows on a stranded hulk
Heavy with sand. We weight the body, close
Its eyes and heave it seaward whence it came,
Where the heel-headed dogfish barks its nose
On Ahab's void and forehead; and the name
Is blocked in yellow chalk.
Sailors, who pitch this portent at the sea
Where dreadnoughts shall confess
Its heel-bent deity,
When you are powerless
To sand-bag this Atlantic bulwark, faced
By the earth-shaker, green, unwearied, chaste
In his steel scales: ask for no Orphean lute
To pluck life back. The guns of the steeled fleet
Recoil and then repeat
The hoarse salute.

II

All you recovered from Poseidon died
With you, my cousin, and the harrowed brine
Is fruitless on the blue beard of the god,
Stretching beyond us to the castles in Spain,
Nantucket's westward haven. To Cape Cod
Guns, cradled on the tide,
Blast the eelgrass about a waterclock
Of bilge and backwash, roil the salt and sand
Lashing earth's scaffold, rock
Our warships in the hand
Of the great God, where time's contrition blues
Whatever it was these Quaker sailors lost
In the mad scramble of their lives. They died
When time was open-eyed,
Wooden and childish; only bones abide

39

There, in the nowhere, where their boats were tossed
Sky-high, where mariners had fabled news
Of IS, the whited monster. What it cost
Them is their secret. In the sperm-whale's slick
I see the Quakers drown and hear their cry:
'If God himself had not been on our side,
If God himself had not been on our side,
When the Atlantic rose against us, why,
Then it had swallowed us up quick.'

III

When the whale's viscera go and the roll
Of its corruption shall overrun this world,
Beyond tree-swept Nantucket and Wood's Hole
And Martha's Vineyard, Sailor, will your sword
Whistle and fall and sink into the fat?
In the great ash-pit of Jehoshaphat
The bones cry for the blood of the white whale,
The fat flukes and whack about its ears,
The death-lance churns into the sanctuary, tears
The gun-blue swingle, heaving like a flail,
And hacks the coiling life out: it works and drags
And rips the sperm-whale's midriff into rags,
Gobbets of blubber spill to wind and weather,
Sailor, and gulls go round the stoven timbers
Where the morning stars sing out together
And thunder shakes the white surf and dismembers
The red flag hammered in the mast-head. Hide,
Our steel, Jonas Messias, in Thy side.

IV

You could cut the brackish winds with a knife
Here in Nantucket, and cast up the time

When the Lord God formed man from the sea's slime
And breathed into his face the breath of life,
And blue-lung'd combers lumbered to the kill.
The Lord survives the rainbow of His will.

The Drunken Fisherman

Wallowing in this bloody sty,
I cast for fish that pleased my eye
(Truly Jehovah's bow suspends
No pots of gold to weight its ends);
Only the blood-mouthed rainbow trout
Rose to my bait. They flopped about . . .

A calendar to tell the day;
A handkerchief to wave away
The gnats; a couch unstuffed with storm
Pouching a bottle in one arm;
A whisky bottle full of worms . . .

Once fishing was a rabbit's foot—
O wind blow cold, O wind blow hot,
Let suns stay in or suns step out:
Life danced a jig on the sperm whale's spout . . .

Now the hot river, ebbing, hauls
Its bloody waters into holes;
A grain of sand inside my shoe
Mimics the moon that might undo
Man and Creation too.

Is there no way to cast my hook
Out of this dynamited brook?

I will catch Christ with a greased worm,
And when the Prince of Darkness stalks
My bloodstream to its Stygian term . . .
On water the Man-Fisher walks.

Between the Porch and the Altar

I

MOTHER AND SON

Meeting his mother makes him lose ten years,
Or is it twenty? Time, no doubt, has ears
That listen to the swallowed serpent, wound
Into its bowels, but he thinks no sound
Is possible before her, he thinks the past
Is settled. It is honest to hold fast
Merely to what one sees with one's own eyes
When the red velvet curves and haunches rise
To blot him from the pretty driftwood fire's
Façade of welcome. Then the son retires
Into the sack and selfhood of the boy
Who clawed through fallen houses of his Troy,
Homely and human only when the flames
Crackle in recollection. Nothing shames
Him more than this uncoiling, counterfeit
Body presented as an idol. It
Is something in a circus, big as life,
The painted dragon, a mother and a wife
With flat glass eyes pushed at him on a stick;
The human mover crawls to make them click.
The forehead of her father's portrait peels
With rosy dryness, and the schoolboy kneels

To ask the benediction of the hand,
Lifted as though to motion him to stand,
Dangling its watch-chain on the Holy Book—
A little golden snake that mouths a hook.

II

ADAM AND EVE

The Farmer sizzles on his shaft all day.
He is content and centuries away
From white-hot Concord, and he stands on guard.
Or is he melting down like sculptured lard?
His hand is crisp and steady on the plough.
I quarrelled with you, but am happy now
To while away my life for your unrest
Of terror. Never to have lived is best;
Man tasted Eve with death. I taste my wife
And children while I hold your hands. I knife
Their names into this elm. What is exempt?
I eye the statue with an awed contempt
And see the puritanical façade
Of the white church that Irish exiles made
For Patrick—that Colonial from Rome
Had magicked the charmed serpents from their home,
As though he were the Piper. Will his breath
Scorch the red dragon of my nerves to death?
By sundown we are on a shore. You walk
A little way before me and I talk,
Half to myself and half aloud. They lied,
My cold-eyed seedy fathers when they died,
Or rather threw their lives away, to fix
Sterile, forbidding nameplates on the bricks
Above a kettle. Jesus rest their souls!
You cry for help. Your market-basket rolls
With all its baking apples in the lake.

You watch the whorish slither of a snake
That chokes a duckling. When we try to kiss,
Our eyes are slits and cringing, and we hiss;
Scales glitter on our bodies as we fall.
The Farmer melts upon his pedestal.

III

KATHERINE'S DREAM

It must have been a Friday. I could hear
The top-floor typist's thunder and the beer
That you had brought in cases hurt my head;
I'd sent the pillows flying from my bed,
I hugged my knees together and I gasped.
The dangling telephone receiver rasped
Like someone in a dream who cannot stop
For breath or logic till his victim drop
To darkness and the sheets. I must have slept,
But still could hear my father who had kept
Your guilty presents but cut off my hair.
He whispers that he really doesn't care
If I am your kept woman all my life,
Or ruin your two children and your wife;
But my dishonour makes him drink. Of course
I'll tell the court the truth for his divorce.
I walk through snow into St. Patrick's yard.
Black nuns with glasses smile and stand on guard
Before a bulkhead in a bank of snow,
Whose charred doors open, as good people go
Inside by twos to the confessor. One
Must have a friend to enter there, but none
Is friendless in this crowd, and the nuns smile.
I stand aside and marvel; for a while
The winter sun is pleasant and it warms
My heart with love for others, but the swarms

44

Of penitents have dwindled. I begin
To cry and ask God's pardon of our sin.
Where are you? You were with me and are gone.
All the forgiven couples hurry on
To dinner and their nights, and none will stop.
I run about in circles till I drop
Against a padlocked bulkhead in a yard
Where faces redden and the snow is hard.

IV

AT THE ALTAR

I sit at a gold table with my girl
Whose eyelids burn with brandy. What a whirl
Of Easter eggs is coloured by the lights,
As the Norwegian dancer's crystalled tights
Flash with her naked leg's high-booted skate,
Like Northern Lights upon my watching plate.
The twinkling steel above me is a star;
I am a fallen Christmas tree. Our car
Races through seven red-lights—then the road
Is unpatrolled and empty, and a load
Of ply-wood with a tail-light makes us slow.
I turn and whisper in her ear. You know
I want to leave my mother and my wife,
You wouldn't have me tied to them for life . . .
Time runs, the windshield runs with stars. The past
Is cities from a train, until at last
Its escalating and black-windowed blocks
Recoil against a Gothic church. The clocks
Are tolling. I am dying. The shocked stones
Are falling like a ton of bricks and bones
That snap and splinter and descend in glass
Before a priest who mumbles through his Mass
And sprinkles holy water; and the Day

Breaks with its lightning on the man of clay,
Dies amara valde. Here the Lord
Is Lucifer in harness: hand on sword,
He watches me for Mother, and will turn
The bier and baby-carriage where I burn.

At the Indian Killer's Grave

*'Here, also, are the veterans of King Philip's War,
who burned villages and slaughtered young and old,
with pious fierceness, while the godly souls through-
out the land were helping them with prayer.'*

HAWTHORNE

Behind King's Chapel what the earth has kept
Whole from the jerking noose of time extends
Its dark enigma to Jehoshaphat;
Or will King Philip plait
The just man's scalp in the wailing valley! Friends,
Blacker than these black stones the subway bends
About the dirty elm roots and the well
For the unchristened infants in the waste
Of the great garden rotten to its roots;
Death, the engraver, puts forward his bone foot
And Grace-with-wings and Time-on-wings compel
All this antique abandon of the disgraced
To face Jehovah's buffets and his ends.

The dusty leaves and frizzled lilacs gear
This garden of the elders with baroque
And prodigal embellishments but smoke,
Settling upon the pilgrims and their grounds,
Espouses and confounds
Their dust with the off-scourings of the town;

46

The libertarian crown
Of England built their mausoleum. Here
A clutter of Bible and weeping willows guards
The stern Colonial magistrates and wards
Of Charles the Second, and the clouds
Weep on the just and unjust as they will,—
For the poor dead cannot see Easter crowds
On Boston Common or the Beacon Hill
Where strangers hold the golden Statehouse dome
For good and always. Where they live is home:
A common with an iron railing: here
Frayed cables wreathe the spreading cenotaph
Of John and Mary Winslow and the laugh
Of Death is hacked in sandstone, in their year.

When we go down this man-hole to the drains,
The doorman barricades us in and out;
We wait upon his pleasure. All about
The pale, sand-coloured, treeless chains
Of T-squared buildings strain
To curb the spreading of the braced terrain;
When you go down this hole, perhaps your pains
Will be rewarded well; no rough-cast house
Will bed and board you in King's Chapel. Here
A public servant putters with a knife
And paints the railing red
Forever, as a mouse
Cracks walnuts by the headstones of the dead
Whose chiselled angels peer
At you, as if their art were long as life.

I ponder on the railing at this park:
Who was the man who sowed the dragon's teeth,
That fabulous or fancied patriarch
Who sowed so ill for his descent, beneath

47

King's Chapel in this underworld and dark?
John, Matthew, Luke and Mark,
Gospel me to the Garden, let me come
Where Mary twists the warlock with her flowers—
Her soul a bridal chamber fresh with flowers
And her whole body an ecstatic womb,
As through the trellis peers the sudden Bridegroom.

In the Cage

The lifers file into the hall,
According to their houses—twos
Of laundered denim. On the wall
A colored fairy tinkles blues
And titters by the balustrade;
Canaries beat their bars and scream.
We come from tunnels where the spade
Pick-axe and hod for plaster steam
In mud and insulation. Here
The Bible-twisting Israelite
Fasts for his Harlem. It is night,
And it is vanity, and age
Blackens the heart of Adam. Fear,
The yellow chirper, beaks its cage.

Mr. Edwards and the Spider

I saw the spiders marching through the air,
Swimming from tree to tree that mildewed day
    In latter August when the hay
    Came creaking to the barn. But where

48

The wind is westerly.
Where gnarled November makes the spiders fly
Into the apparitions of the sky,
They purpose nothing but their ease and die
Urgently beating east to sunrise and the sea;

What are we in the hands of the great God?
It was in vain you set up thorn and briar
    In battle array against the fire
    And treason cracking in your blood;
        For the wild thorns grow tame
And will do nothing to oppose the flame;
Your lacerations tell the losing game
You play against a sickness past your cure.
How will the hands be strong? How will the heart endure?

A very little thing, a little worm,
Or hourglass-blazoned spider, it is said,
    Can kill a tiger. Will the dead
    Hold up his mirror and affirm
        Against the four winds the smell
And flash of his authority? It's well
If God who holds you to the pit of hell,
Much as one holds a spider, will destroy,
Baffle and dissipate your soul. As a small boy

On Windsor Marsh, I saw the spider die
When thrown into the bowels of fierce fire:
    There's no long struggle, no desire
    To get up on its feet and fly—
        It stretches out its feet
And dies. This is the sinner's last retreat;
Yes, and no strength exerted on the heat
Then sinews the abolished will, when sick
And full of burning, it will whistle on a brick.

But who can plumb the sinking of that soul?
Josiah Hawley, picture yourself cast
  Into a brick-kiln where the blast
  Fans your quick vitals to a coal—
    If measured by a glass,
How long would it seem burning! Let there pass
A minute, ten, ten trillion; but the blaze
Is infinite, eternal: this is death,
To die and know it. This is the Black Widow, death.

from
LIFE STUDIES

Beyond the Alps

*(On the train from Rome to Paris, 1950, the year when Pius XII
defined the dogma of Mary's bodily assumption.)*

Reading how even the Swiss had thrown the sponge
in once again and Everest was still
unscaled, I watched our Paris pullman lunge
mooning across the fallow Alpine snow.
O bella Roma! I saw our stewards go
forward on tiptoe banging on their gongs.
Man changed to landscape. Much against my will,
I left the City of God where it belongs.
There the skirt-mad Mussolini unfurled
the eagle of Caesar. He was one of us
only, pure prose. I envy the conspicuous
waste of our grandparents on their grand tours—
long-haired Victorian sages accepted the universe,
while breezing on their trust funds through the world.

When the Vatican made Mary's Assumption dogma,
the crowds at San Pietro screamed *Papa.*
The Holy Father dropped his shaving glass,
and listened. His electric razor purred,
his pet canary chirped on his left hand.
The lights of science couldn't hold a candle
to Mary risen—at one miraculous stroke,
angel-wing'd, gorgeous as a jungle bird!
But who believed this? Who could understand?
Pilgrims still kissed Saint Peter's brazen sandal.
The Duce's lynched, bare, booted skull still spoke.
God herded his people to the *coup de grâce—*
the costumed Switzers sloped their pikes to push,
O Pius, through the monstrous human crush. . . .

I thought of Ovid. For in Caesar's eyes
that tomcat had the Number of the Beast,
and now where Turkey faces the red east,
and the twice-stormed Crimean spit, he lies.
Rome asked for poets. At her beck and call,
came Lucan, Tacitus and Juvenal,
the *black republicans* who tore the tits
and bowels of the Mother Wolf to bits.
Killer and army-commander waved the rod
of empire over the Caesars' salvaged bog . . .
'Imperial Tiber, Oh my yellow dog,
black earth by the black Roman sea, I lie
with the boy-crazy daughter of the God.
il duce Augusto. I shall never die.'

Our mountain-climbing train had come to earth.
Tired of the querulous hush-hush of the wheels,
the blear-eyed ego kicking in my berth
lay still, and saw Apollo plant his heels
on terra firma through the morning's thigh . . .
each backward, wasted Alp, a Parthenon,
fire-branded socket of the Cyclop's eyes.
There are no tickets for that altitude
once held by Hellsa, when the Goddess stood,
prince, pope, philosopher and golden bough,
pure mind and murder at the scything prow—
Minerva, the miscarriage of the brain.

Now Paris, our black classic, breaking up
like killer kings on an Etruscan cup.

Inauguration Day: January 1953

The snow had buried Stuyvesant.
The subways drummed the vaults. I heard
the El's green girders charge on Third,
Manhattan's truss of adamant,
that groaned in ermine, slummed on want. . . .
Cyclonic zero of the Word,
God of our armies, who interred
Cold Harbour's blue immortals, Grant!
Horseman, your sword is in the groove!
Ice, ice. Our wheels no longer move;
Look, the fixed stars, all just alike
as lack-land atoms, split apart,
and the Republic summons Ike,
the mausoleum in her heart.

A Mad Negro Soldier Confined at Munich

'We're all Americans, except the Doc,
a Kraut DP, who kneels and bathes my eye.
The boys who floored me, two black maniacs try
to pat my hands. Rounds, rounds! Why punch the clock?

In Munich the zoo's rubble fumes with cats;
hoydens with air-guns prowl the Koenigsplatz,
and pink the pigeons on the mustard spire.
Who but my girl-friend set the town on fire?

Cat-houses talk cold turkey to my guards;
I found my *fraulein* stitching outing shirts
in the black forest of the colored wards—
lieutenants squawked like chickens in her skirts.

Her German language made my arteries harden—
I've no annuity from the pay we blew.
I chartered an aluminum canoe,
I had her six times in the English Garden.

Oh mama, mama, like a trolley-pole
sparking at contact, her electric shock—
the power-house! . . . The doctor calls our roll—
no knives, no forks. We file before the clock,

and fancy minnows, slaves of habit, shoot
like starlight through their air-conditioned bowl.
It's time for feeding. Each subnormal boot-
black heart is pulsing to its ant-egg dole.'

My Last Afternoon with Uncle Devereux Winslow

(*1922: the stone porch of my Grandfather's summer house*)

I

'I won't go with you. I want to stay with Grandpa!'
That's how I threw cold water
on my Mother's and Father's
watery martini pipe dreams at Sunday dinner.
Fontainebleau, Mattapoisett, Puget Sound . . .
Nowhere was anywhere after a summer
at my Grandfather's farm.
Diamond-pointed, athirst and Norman,
its alley of poplars
paraded from Grandmother's rose garden
to a scarey stand of virgin pine,
scrub, and paths forever pioneering.

One afternoon in 1922,
I sat on the stone porch, looking through
screens as black-grained as drifting coal.
Tockytock, tockytock
clumped our Alpine, Edwardian cuckoo clock,
slung with strangled, wooden game.
Our farmer was cementing a root-house under the hill.
One of my hands was cool on a pile
of black earth, the other warm
on a pile of lime. All about me
were the works of my Grandfather's hands:
snapshots of his *Liberty Bell* silver mine,
his high school at *Stukkert am Neckar*,
stogie-brown beams, fools'-gold nuggets,
octagonal red tiles,
sweaty with a secret dank, crummy with an ant-stale,
a Rocky Mountain chaise longue,
its legs, shellacked saplings.
A pastel-pale Huckleberry Finn
fished with a broom straw in a basin
hollowed out of a millstone.
Like my Grandfather, the décor
was manly, comfortable,
overbearing, disproportioned.

What were those sunflowers? Pumpkins floating shoulder-
      high?
It was the sunset on Sadie and Nellie
bearing pitchers of ice-tea,
oranges, lemons, mint, and peppermints,
and the jug of shandygaff,
which Grandpa made by blending half and half
yeasty, wheezing homemade sarsaparilla with beer.
The farm, entitled *Char-de-sa*
in the Social Register,

was named for my Grandfather's children:
Charlotte, Devereux, and Sarah.
No one had died there in my lifetime . . .
Only Cinder, our Scottie puppy
paralysed from gobbling toads.
I sat mixing black earth and lime.

II

I was five and a half.
My formal pearl grey shorts
had been worn for three minutes.
My perfection was the Olympian
poise of my models in the imperishable autumn
display windows
of Roger Pett's boys' store below the State House
in Boston. Distorting drops of water
pinpricked my face in the basin's mirror.
I was a stuffed toucan
with a bibulous, multicoloured beak.

III

Up in the air
by the lakeview window in the billiards-room,
lurid in the doldrums of the sunset hour,
my Great Aunt Sarah
was learning *Samson and Delilah*.
She thundered on the keyboard of her dummy piano
with gauze curtains like a boudoir table,
accordionlike yet soundless.
It had been bought to spare the nerves
of my Grandmother,
tone-deaf, quick as a cricket,
now needing a fourth for 'Auction',
and casting a thirsty eye

on Aunt Sarah, risen like the phoenix
from her bed of troublesome snacks and Tauchnitz classics.

Forty years earlier,
twenty, auburn headed,
grasshopper notes of genius!
Family gossip says Aunt Sarah
tilted her archaic Athenian nose
and jilted an Astor.
Each morning she practised
on the grand piano at Symphony Hall,
deathlike in the off-season summer—
its naked Greek statues draped with purple
like the saints in Holy Week. . . .
On the recital day, she failed to appear.

IV

I picked with a clean finger nail at the blue anchor
on my sailor blouse washed white as a spinnaker.
What in the world was I wishing?
. . . A sail-coloured horse browsing in the bulrushes . . .
A fluff of the west wind puffing
my blouse, kiting me over our seven chimneys,
troubling the waters. . . .
As small as sapphires were the ponds: *Quittacus*, *Snippituit*,
and *Assawompset*, halved by 'the island',
where my Uncle's duck blind
floated in a barrage of smoke-clouds.
Double-barrelled shotguns
stuck out like bundles of baby crow-bars.
A single sculler in a camouflaged kayak
was quacking to the decoys. . . .

At the cabin between the waters,

the nearest windows were already boarded.
Uncle Devereux was closing camp for the winter.
As if posed for 'the engagement photograph',
he was wearing his severe
war-uniform of a volunteer Canadian officer.
Daylight from the doorway riddled his student posters,
tacked helter-skelter on the walls as raw as a board-walk.
Mr Punch, a water melon in hockey tights,
was tossing off a decanter of Scotch.
La Belle France in a red, white and blue toga
was accepting the arm of her 'protector',
the ingenu and porcine Edward VII.
The pre-war music hall belles
had goose necks, glorious signatures, beauty-moles,
and coils of hair like rooster tails.
The finest poster was two or three young men in khaki
    kilts
being bushwhacked on the veldt—
They were almost life-sized. . . .

My Uncle was dying at twenty-nine.
'You are behaving like children,'
said my Grandfather,
when my Uncle and Aunt left their three baby daughters,
and sailed for Europe on a last honeymoon . . .
I cowered in terror.
I wasn't a child at all—
unseen and all-seeing, I was Agrippina
in the Golden House of Nero. . . .
Near me was the white measuring-door
my Grandfather had pencilled with my Uncle's heights.
In 1911, he had stopped growing at just six feet.
While I sat on the tiles,
and dug at the anchor on my sailor blouse,
Uncle Devereux stood behind me.

He was as brushed as Bayard, our riding horse.
His face was putty.
His blue coat and white trousers
grew sharper and straighter.
His coat was a blue jay's tail,
his trousers were solid cream from the top of the bottle.
He was animated, hierarchical,
like a ginger snap man in a clothes-press.
He was dying of the incurable Hodgkin's disease. . . .
My hands were warm, then cool, on the piles
of earth and lime,
a black pile and a white pile. . . .
Come winter,
Uncle Devereux would blend to the one colour.

Commander Lowell 1888—1949

There were no undesirables or girls in my set,
when I was a boy at Mattapoisett—
only Mother, still her Father's daughter.
Her voice was still electric
with a hysterical, unmarried panic,
when she read to me from the Napoleon book.
Long-nosed Marie Louise
Hapsburg in the frontispiece
had a downright Boston bashfulness,
where she groveled to Bonaparte, who scratched his navel,
and bolted his food—just my seven years tall!
And I, bristling and manic,
skulked in the attic,
and got two hundred French generals by name,
from *A* to *V*—from Augereau to Vandamme.
I used to dope myself asleep,
naming those unpronounceables like sheep.

Having a naval officer
for my Father was nothing to shout
about to the summer colony as 'Matt'.
He wasn't at all 'serious',
when he showed up on the golf course,
wearing a blue serge jacket and numbly cut
white ducks he'd bought
at a Pearl Harbour commissariat . . .
and took four shots with his putter to sink his putt.
'Bob,' they said, 'golf's a game you really ought to know how
    to play,
if you play at all.'
They wrote him off as 'naval',
naturally supposed his sport was sailing.
Poor Father, his training was engineering!
Cheerful and cowed
among the seadogs at the Sunday yacht club,
he was never one of the crowd.

'Anchors aweigh,' Daddy boomed in his bathtub,
'Anchors aweigh,'
when Lever Brothers offered to pay
him double what the Navy paid.
I nagged for his dress sword with gold braid,
and cringed because Mother, new
caps on her teeth, was born anew
at forty. With seamanlike celerity,
Father left the Navy,
and deeded Mother his property.

He was soon fired. Year after year,
he still hummed 'Anchors aweigh' in the tub—
whenever he left a job,
he bought a smarter car.
Father's last employer

was Scudder, Stevens and Clark, Investment Advisers,
himself his only client.
While Mother dragged to bed alone,
read Menninger,
and grew more and more suspicious,
he grew defiant.
Night after night,
a la clarté déserte de sa lampe,
he slid his ivory Annapolis slide rule
across a pad of graphs—
piker speculations! In three years
he squandered sixty thousand dollars.

Smiling on all,
Father was once successful enough to be lost
in the mob of ruling-class Bostonians.
As early as 1928,
he owned a house converted to oil,
and redecorated by the architect
of St Mark's School. . . . Its main effect
was a drawing room, 'longitudinal as Versailles',
its ceiling, roughened with oatmeal, was blue as the sea.
And once
nineteen, the youngest ensign in his class,
he was 'the old man' of a gunboat on the Yangtze.

Terminal days at Beverly Farms

At Beverly Farms, a portly, uncomfortable boulder
bulked in the garden's centre—
an irregular Japanese touch.
After his Bourbon 'old fashioned', Father,
bronzed, breezy, a shade too ruddy,

swayed as if on deck-duty
under his six-pointed star-lantern—
last July's birthday present.
He smiled his oval Lowell smile,
he wore his cream gabardine dinner-jacket,
and indigo cummerbund.
His head was efficient and hairless,
his newly dieted figure was vitally trim.

Father and Mother moved to Beverly Farms
to be a two minute walk from the station,
half an hour by train from the Boston doctors.
They had no sea-view,
but sky-blue tracks of the commuters' railroad shone
like a double-barrelled shotgun
through the scarlet late August sumac,
multiplying like cancer
at their garden's border.

Father had had two coronaries.
He still treasured underhand economies,
but his best friend was his little black *Chevie*,
garaged like a sacrificial steer
with gilded hooves,
yet sensationally sober,
and with less side than an old dancing pump.
The local dealer, a 'buccaneer',
had been bribed a 'king's ransom'
to quickly deliver a car without chrome.

Each morning at eight-thirty,
inattentive and beaming,
loaded with his 'calc' and 'trig' books,
his clipper ship statistics,
and his ivory slide-rule,

Father stole off with the *Chevie*
to loaf in the Maritime Museum at Salem.
He called the curator
'the commander of the Swiss Navy'

Father's death was abrupt and unprotesting.
His vision was still twenty-twenty.
After a morning of anxious, repetitive smiling,
his last words to Mother were:
'I feel awful.'

Father's Bedroom

In my Father's bedroom:
blue threads as thin
as pen writing on the bedspread,
blue dots on the curtains,
a blue kimono,
Chinese sandals with blue plush straps.
The broad-planked floor
had a sandpapered neatness.
The clear glass bed-lamp
with a white doily shade
was still raised a few
inches by resting on volume two
of Lafcadio Hearn's
Glimpses of unfamiliar Japan.
Its warped olive cover
was punished like a rhinoceros hide.
In the flyleaf:
'Robbie from Mother.'
Years later in the same hand:
'This book has had hard usage

On the Yangtze River, China.
It was left under an open
porthole in a storm.'

Sailing Home From Rapallo
(February 1954)

Your nurse could only speak Italian,
but after twenty minutes I could imagine your final week,
and tears ran down my cheeks. . . .

When I embarked from Italy with my Mother's body,
the whole shoreline of the *Golfo di Genova*
was breaking into fiery flower.
The crazy yellow and azure sea-sleds
blasting like jack hammers across
the *spumante*-bubbling wake of our liner,
recalled the clashing colours of my Ford.
Mother travelled first-class in the hold,
her *Risorgimento* black and gold casket
was like Napoleon's at the *Invalides*. . . .

While the passengers were tanning
on the Mediterranean in deck-chairs,
our family cemetery in Dunbarton
lay under the White Mountains
in the sub-zero weather.
The graveyard's soil was changing to stone—
so many of its deaths had been midwinter.
Dour and dark against the blinding snowdrifts,
its black brook and fir trunks were as smooth as masts.
A fence of iron spear-hafts
black-bordered its mostly Colonial grave-slates.

The only 'unhistoric' soul to come here
was Father, now buried beneath his recent
unweathered, pink-veined slice of marble.
Even the Latin of his Lowell motto:
Occasionem cognosce,
seemed too businesslike and pushing here,
where the burning cold illuminated
the hewn inscriptions of Mother's relatives:
twenty or thirty Winslows and Starks.
Frost had given their names a diamond edge. . . .

In the grandiloquent lettering on Mother's coffin,
Lowell had been misspelled *LOVEL*.
The corpse
was wrapped like *panetone* in Italian tinfoil.

Waking in the Blue

The night attendant, a B.U. sophomore,
rouses from the mare's-nest of his drowsy head
propped on *The Meaning of Meaning*.
He catwalks down our corridor.
Azure day
makes my agonized blue window bleaker.
Crows maunder on the petrified fairway.
Absence! My heart grows tense
as though a harpoon were sparring for the kill.
(This is the house for the 'mentally ill'.)

What use is my sense of humour?
I grin at 'Stanley', now sunk in his sixties,
once a Harvard all-American fullback,
(if such were possible!)

still hoarding the build of a boy in his twenties,
as he soaks, a ramrod
with the muscle of a seal
in his long tub,
vaguely urinous from the Victorian plumbing.
A kingly granite profile in a crimson golf-cap,
worn all day, all night,
he thinks only of his figure,
of slimming on sherbert and ginger ale—
more cut off from words than a seal.

This is the way day breaks in Bowditch Hall at McLeans;
the hooded night lights bring out 'Bobbie',
Porcellian '29,
a replica of Louis XVI
without the wig—
redolent and roly-poly as a sperm whale,
as he swashbuckles about in his birthday suit
and horses at chairs.

These victorious figures of bravado ossified young.

In between the limits of day,
hours and hours go by under the crew haircuts
and slightly too little nonsensical twinkle
of the Roman Catholic attendants.
(There are no Mayflower
screwballs in the Catholic Church.)

After a hearty New England breakfast,
I weigh two hundred pounds
this morning. Cock of the walk,
I strut in my turtle-necked French sailor's jersey
before the metal shaving mirrors,
and see the shaky future grow familiar

in the pinched, indigenous faces
of these thoroughbred mental cases,
twice my age and half my weight.
We are all old-timers,
each of us holds a locked razor.

Home After Three Months Away

Gone now the baby's nurse,
a lioness who ruled the roost
and made the Mother cry.
She used to tie
gobbets of porkrind in bowknots of gauze—
three months they hung like soggy toast
on our eight foot magnolia tree,
and helped the English sparrows
weather a Boston winter.

Three months, three months!
Is Richard now himself again?
Dimpled with exaltation,
my daughter holds her levee in the tub.
Our noses rub,
each of us pats a stringy lock of hair—
they tell me nothing's gone.
Though I am forty-one,
not forty now, the time I put away
was child's play. After thirteen weeks
my child still dabs her cheeks
to start me shaving. When
we dress her in her sky-blue corduroy,
she changes to a boy,
and floats my shaving brush

and washcloth in the flush. . . .
Dearest, I cannot loiter here
in lather like a polar bear.

Recuperating, I neither spin nor toil.
Three stories down below,
a choreman tends our coffin's length of soil,
and seven horizontal tulips blow.
Just twelve months ago,
these flowers were pedigreed
imported Dutchmen, now no one need
distinguish them from weed.
Bushed by the late spring snow,
they cannot meet
another year's snowballing enervation.

I keep no rank nor station.
Cured, I am frizzled, stale and small.

Memories of West Street and Lepke

Only teaching on Tuesdays, book-worming
in pajamas fresh from the washer each morning,
I hog a whole house on Boston's
'hardly passionate Marlborough Street',
where even the man
scavenging filth in the back alley trash cans,
has two children, a beach wagon, a helpmate,
and is 'a young Republican'.
I have a nine months' daughter,
young enough to be my granddaughter.
Like the sun she rises in her flame-flamingo infants' wear.

These are the tranquillized *Fifties*,
and I am forty. Ought I to regret my seedtime?
I was a fire-breathing Catholic C.O.,
and made my manic statement,
telling off the state and president, and then
sat waiting sentence in the bull pen
beside a negro boy with curlicues
of marijuana in his hair.

Given a year,
I walked on the roof of the West Street Jail, a short
enclosure like my school soccer court,
and saw the Hudson River once a day
through sooty clothesline entanglements
and bleaching khaki tenements.
Strolling, I yammered metaphysics with Abramowitz,
a jaundice-yellow ('it's really tan')
and fly-weight pacifist,
so vegetarian,
he wore rope shoes and preferred fallen fruit.
He tried to convert Bioff and Brown,
the Hollywood pimps, to his diet.
Hairy, muscular, suburban,
wearing chocolate double-breasted suits,
they blew their tops and beat him black and blue.

I was so out of things, I'd never heard
of the Jehovah's Witnesses.
'Are you a C.O.?' I asked a fellow jailbird.
'No,' he answered, 'I'm a J.W.'
He taught me the hospital 'tuck',
and pointed out the T-shirted back
of *Murder Incorporated's* Czar Lepke,
there piling towels on a rack,
or dawdling off to his little segregated cell full

of things forbidden the common man:
a portable radio, a dresser, two toy American
flags tied together with a ribbon of Easter palm.
Flabby, bald, lobotomized,
he drifted in a sheepish calm,
where no agonizing reappraisal
jarred his concentration on the electric chair—
hanging like an oasis in his air
of lost connections . . .

Man and Wife

Tamed by *Miltown*, we lie on Mother's bed;
the rising sun in war paint dyes us red;
in broad daylight her gilded bed-posts shine,
abandoned, almost Dionysian.
At last the trees are green on Marlborough Street,
blossoms on our magnolia ignite
the morning with their murderous five days' white.
All night I've held your hand,
as if you had
a fourth time faced the kingdom of the mad—
its hackneyed speech, its homicidal eye—
and dragged me home alive. . . . Oh my *Petite*,
clearest of all God's creatures, still all air and nerve:
you were in your twenties, and I,
once hand on glass
and heart in mouth,
outdrank the Rahvs in the heat
of Greenwich Village, fainting at your feet—
too boiled and shy
and poker-faced to make a pass,

while the shrill verve
of your invective scorched the traditional South.

Now twelve years later, you turn your back.
Sleepless, you hold
your pillow to your hollows like a child,
your old-fashioned tirade—
loving, rapid, merciless—
breaks like the Atlantic Ocean on my head.

'To Speak of the Woe That is In Marriage'

*'It is the future generation that presses into being by means of these
exuberant feelings and supersensible soap bubbles of ours.'*

SCHOPENHAUER

'The hot night makes us keep our bedroom windows open.
Our magnolia blossoms. Life begins to happen.
My hopped up husband drops his home disputes,
and hits the streets to cruise for prostitutes,
free-lancing out along the razor's edge.
This screwball might kill his wife, then take the pledge.
Oh the monotonous meanness of his lust. . . .
It's the injustice . . . he is so unjust—
whiskey-blind, swaggering home at five.
My only thought is how to keep alive.
What makes him tick? Each night now I tie
ten dollars and his car key to my thigh. . . .
Gored by the climacteric of his want,
he stalls above me like an elephant.'

Skunk Hour

(for Elizabeth Bishop)

Nautilus Island's hermit
heiress still lives through winter in her Spartan cottage;
her sheep still graze above the sea.
Her son's a bishop. Her farmer
is first selectman in our village,
she's in her dotage.

Thirsting for
the hierarchic privacy
of Queen Victoria's century,
she buys up all
the eyesores facing her shore,
and lets them fall.

The season's ill—
we've lost our summer millionaire,
who seemed to leap from an L. L. Bean
catalogue. His nine-knot yawl
was auctioned off to lobstermen.
A red fox stain covers Blue Hill.

And now our fairy
decorator brightens his shop for fall,
his fishnet's filled with orange cork,
orange, his cobbler's bench and awl,
there is no money in his work,
he'd rather marry.

One dark night,
my Tudor Ford climbed the hill's skull,
I watched for love-cars. Lights turned down,

they lay together, hull to hull,
where the graveyard shelves on the town. . . .
My mind's not right.

A car radio bleats,
'Love, O careless Love . . .' I hear
my ill-spirit sob in each blood cell,
as if my hand were at its throat . . .
I myself am hell,
nobody's here—

only skunks, that search
in the moonlight for a bite to eat.
They march on their soles up Main Street:
white stripes, moonstruck eyes' red fire
under the chalk-dry and spar spire
of the Trinitarian Church.

I stand on top
of our back steps and breathe the rich air—
a mother skunk with her column of kittens swills the
        garbage pail
She jabs her wedge head in a cup
of sour cream, drops her ostrich tail,
and will not scare.

from
FOR THE UNION DEAD

Water

It was a Maine lobster town—
Each morning boatloads of hands
pushed off for granite
quarries on the islands,

and left dozens of bleak
white frame houses stuck
like oyster shells
on a hill of rock,

and below us, the sea lapped
the raw little match-stick
mazes of a weir
where the fish for bait were trapped.

Remember? We sat on a slab of rock.
From this distance in time,
it seems the color
of iris, rotting and turning purpler,

but it was only
the usual gray rock
turning the usual green
when drenched by the sea.

The sea drenched the rock
at our feet all day,
and kept tearing away
flake after flake.

One night you dreamed
you were a mermaid clinging to a wharf-pile,

and trying to pull
off the barnacles with your hands.
We wished our two souls
might return like gulls
to the rock. In the end,
the water was too cold for us.

The Old Flame

My old flame, my wife!
Remember our lists of birds?
One morning last summer, I drove
by our house in Maine. It was still
on top of its hill—
Now a red ear of Indian maize
was splashed on the door.
Old Glory with thirteen stripes
hung on a pole. The clapboard
was old-red schoolhouse red.

Inside, a new landlord,
a new wife, a new broom!
Atlantic seaboard antique shop
pewter and plunder
shone in each room.

A new frontier!
No running next door
now to phone the sheriff
for his taxi to Bath
and the State Liquor Store!

No one saw your ghostly
imaginary lover
stare through the window,
and tighten
the scarf at his throat.

Health to the new people,
health to their flag, to their old
restored house on the hill!
Everything had been swept bare,
furnished, garnished and aired.

Everything's changed for the best—
how quivering and fierce we were,
there snowbound together,
simmering like wasps
in our tent of books!

Poor ghost, old love, speak
with your old voice
of flaming insight
that kept us awake all night.
In one bed and apart,

we heard the plow
groaning up hill—
a red light, then a blue,
as it tossed off the snow
to the side of the road.

Middle Age

Now the midwinter grind
is on me, New York
drills through my nerves,
as I walk
the chewed-up streets.

At forty-five,
what next, what next?
At every corner,
I meet my Father,
my age, still alive.

Father, forgive me
my injuries,
as I forgive
those I
have injured!

You never climbed
Mount Sion, yet left
dinosaur
death-steps on the crust,
where I must walk.

Fall 1961

Back and forth, back and forth
goes the tock, tock, tock
of the orange, bland, ambassadorial
face of the moon
on the grandfather clock.

All autumn, the chafe and jar
of nuclear war;
we have talked our extinction to death.
I swim like a minnow
Behind my studio window.

Our end drifts nearer,
the moon lifts,
radiant with terror.
The state
is a diver under a glass bell.

A father's no shield
for his child.
We are like a lot of wild
spiders crying together,
but without tears.

Nature holds up a mirror.
One swallow makes a summer.
It's easy to tick
Off the minutes,
but the clockhands stick.

Back and forth!
Back and forth, back and forth—
my one point of rest
is the orange and black
oriole's swinging nest!

Eye and Tooth

My whole eye was sunset red,
the old cut cornea throbbed,
I saw things darkly,
as through an unwashed goldfish globe.

I lay all day on my bed.
I chain-smoked through the night,
learning to flinch
at the flash of the matchlight.

Outside, the summer rain,
a simmer of rot and renewal,
fell in pinpricks.
Even new life is fuel.

My eyes throb.
Nothing can dislodge
the house with my first tooth
noosed in a knot to the doorknob.

Nothing can dislodge
the triangular blotch
of rot on the red roof,
a cedar hedge, or the shade of a hedge.

No ease from the eye
of the sharp-shinned hawk in the birdbook there,
with reddish brown buffalo hair
on its shanks, one ascetic talon

clasping the abstract imperial sky.
It says:

an eye for an eye,
a tooth for a tooth.

No ease for the boy at the keyhole,
his telescope,
when the women's white bodies flashed
in the bathroom. Young, my eyes began to fail.

Nothing! No oil
for the eye, nothing to pour
on those waters or flames.
I am tired. Everyone's tired of my turmoil.

Law

Under one law,
or two,
to lie unsleeping,
still sleeping on the battlefield . . .

On Sunday mornings,
I used to foray
bass-plugging out of season on
the posted reservoirs.

Outside the law.
At every bend I saw
only the looping shore
of nature's monotonous backlash.

The same. The same.
Then once, in a flash,

fresh ground, though trodden,
a man-made landscape.

A Norman canal
shot through razored green lawns;
black reflecting water arched
little sky-hung bridges of unhewn stone—

outside the law:
black, gray, green and blue,
water, stone, grass and sky,
and each unique set stone!

The Public Garden

Burnished, burned-out, still burning as the year
you lead me to our stamping ground.
The city and its cruising cars surround
the Public Garden. All's alive—
the children crowding home from school at five,
punting a football in the bricky air,
the sailors and their pick-ups under trees
with Latin labels. And the jaded flock
of swanboats paddles to its dock.
The park is drying.
Dead leaves thicken to a ball
inside the basin of a fountain, where
the heads of four stone lions stare
and suck on empty fawcets. Night
deepens. From the arched bridge, we see
the shedding park-bound mallards, how they keep
circling and diving in the lanternlight,
searching for something hidden in the muck.

And now the moon, earth's friend, that cared so much
for us, and cared so little, comes again—
always a stranger! As we walk,
it lies like chalk
over the waters. Everything's aground.
Remember summer! Bubbles filled
the fountain, and we splashed. We drowned
in Eden, while Jehovah's grass-green lyre
was rustling all about us in the leaves
that gurgled by us, turning upside down . . .
The fountain's failing waters flash around
the garden. Nothing catches fire.

Returning

Homecoming to the sheltered little resort,
where the members of my gang
are bald-headed, in business,
and the dogs still know me by my smell . . .
It's rather a dead town
after my twenty years' mirage.

Long awash,
breaking myself against the surf,
touching bottom, rushed
by the green go-light
of those nervous waters, I found
my exhaustion, the light of the world.

Nothing is deader than this small town main street,
where the venerable elm sickens, and hardens
with tarred cement, where no leaf
is born, or falls, or resists till winter.

But I remember its former fertility,
how everything came out clearly
in the hour of credulity
and young summer, when this street
was already somewhat overshaded,
and here at the altar of surrender,
I met you,
the death of thirst in my brief flesh.

That was the first growth,
the heir of all my minutes,
the victim of every ramification—
more and more it grew green, and gave too much shelter.

And now at my homecoming,
the barked elms stand up like sticks along the street.
I am a foot taller than when I left,
and cannot see the dirt at my feet.

Yet sometimes I catch my vague mind
circling with a glazed eye
for a name without a face, or a face without a name,
and at every step,
I startle them. They start up,
dog-eared, bald as baby birds.

The Drinker

The man is killing time—there's nothing else.
No help now from the fifth of Bourbon
chucked helter-skelter into the river,
even its cork sucked under.

Stubbed before-breakfast cigarettes
burn bull's-eyes on the bedside table;
a plastic tumbler of alka seltzer
champagnes in the bathroom.

No help from his body, the whale's
warm-hearted blubber, foundering down
leagues of ocean, gasping whiteness.
The barbed hooks fester. The lines snap tight.

When he looks for neighbors, their names blur in the window,
his distracted eye sees only glass sky.
His despair has the galvanized color
of the mop and water in the galvanized bucket.

Once she was close to him
as water to the dead metal.

He looks at her engagements inked on her calendar.
A list of indictments.
At the numbers in her thumbed black telephone book.
A quiver full of arrows.

Her absence hisses like steam,
the pipes sing . . .
even corroded metal somehow functions.
He snores in his iron lung,

and hears the voice of Eve,
beseeching freedom from the Garden's
perfect and ponderous bubble. No voice
outsings the serpent's flawed, euphoric hiss.

The cheese wilts in the rat-trap,
the milk turns to junket in the cornflakes bowl,

car keys and razor blades
shine in an ashtray.

Is he killing time? Out on the street,
two cops on horseback clop through the April rain
to check the parking meter violations—
their oilskins yellow as forsythia.

Tenth Muse

Tenth Muse, Oh my heart-felt Sloth,
how often now you come to my bed,
thin as a canvas in your white and red
check dresses like a table cloth,
my Dearest, settling like my shroud!

Yes, yes, I ought to remember Moses
jogging down on his mule from the Mount
with the old law, the old mistake,
safe in his saddlebags, and chiselled
on the stones we cannot bear or break.

Here waiting, here waiting for an answer
from this malignant surf of unopened letters,
always reaching land too late,
as fact and abstraction accumulate,
and the signature fades from the paper—

I like to imagine it must have been simpler
in the days of Lot,
or when Greek and Roman picturebook
gods sat combing their golden beards,
each on his private hill or mountain.

But I suppose even God was born
too late to trust the old religion—
all those settings out
that never left the ground,
beginning in wisdom, dying in doubt.

July in Washington

The stiff spokes of this wheel
touch the sore spots of the earth.

On the Potomac, swan-white
power launches keep breasting the sulphurous wave.

Otters slide and dive and slick back their hair,
raccoons clean their meat in the creek.

On the circles, green statues ride like South American
liberators above the breeding vegetation—

prongs and spearheads of some equatorial
backland that will inherit the globe.

The elect, the elected . . . they come here bright as dimes,
and die dishevelled and soft.

We cannot name their names, or number their dates—
circle on circle, like rings on a tree—

but we wish the river had another shore,
some further range of delectable mountains,

distant hills powdered blue as a girl's eyelid.
It seems the least little shove would land us there,

that only the slightest repugnance of our bodies
we no longer control could drag us back.

Soft Wood

(FOR HARRIET WINSLOW)

Sometimes I have supposed seals
must live as long the Scholar Gypsy.
Even in their barred pond at the zoo they are happy,
and no sunflower turns
more delicately to the sun
without a wincing of the will.

Here too in Maine things bend to the wind forever.
After two years away, one must get used
to the painted soft wood staying bright and clean,
to the air blasting an all-white wall whiter,
as it blows through curtain and screen
touched with salt and evergreen.

The green juniper berry spills crystal-clear gin,
and even the hot water in the bathtub
is more than water,
and rich with the scouring effervescence
of something healing,
the illimitable salt.

Things last, but sometimes for days here
only children seem fit to handle children,

and there is no utility or inspiration
in the wind smashing without direction.
The fresh paint
on the captains' houses hides softer wood.

Their square-riggers used to whiten
the four corners of the globe,
but it's no consolation to know
the possessors seldom outlast the possessions,
once warped and mothered by their touch.
Shed skin will never fit another wearer.

Yet the seal pack will bark past my window
summer after summer.
This is the season
when our friends may and will die daily.
Surely the lives of the old
are briefer than the young.
Harriet Winslow, who owned this house,
was more to me than my mother.
I think of you far off in Washington,
breathing in the heat wave
and air-conditioning, knowing
each drug that numbs alerts another nerve to pain.

The Flaw

A seal swims like a poodle through the sheet
of blinding salt. A country graveyard, here
and there a rock, and here and there a pine,
throbs on the essence of the gasoline.
Some mote, some eye-flaw, wobbles in the heat,
hair-thin, hair-dark, the fragment of a hair—

a noose, a question? All is possible;
if there's free will, it's something like this hair,
inside my eye, outside my eye, yet free,
airless as grace, if the good God . . . I see.
Our bodies quiver. In this rustling air,
all's possible, all's unpredictable.

Old wives and husbands! Look, their gravestones wait
in couples with the names and half the date—
one future and one freedom. In a flash,
I see us whiten into skeletons,
our eager, sharpened cries, a pair of stones,
cutting like shark-fins through the boundless wash.

Two walking cobwebs, almost bodiless,
crossed paths here once, kept house, and lay in beds.
Your fingertips once touched my fingertips
and set us tingling through a thousand threads.
Poor pulsing *Fête Champêtre!* The summer slips
between our fingers into nothingness.

We too lean forward, as the heat waves roll
over our bodies, grown insensible,
ready to dwindle off into the soul,
two motes or eye-flaws, the invisible . . .
Hope of the hopeless launched and cast adrift
on the great flaw that gives the final gift.

Dear Figure curving like a questionmark,
how will you hear my answer in the dark?

For the Union Dead

'*Relinquunt Omnia Servare Rem Publicam.*'

The old South Boston Aquarium stands
in a Sahara of snow now. Its broken windows are boarded.
The bronze weathervane cod has lost half its scales.
The airy tanks are dry.

Once my nose crawled like a snail on the glass;
my hand tingled
to burst the bubbles
drifting from the noses of the cowed, compliant fish.

My hand draws back. I often sigh still
for the dark downward and vegetating kingdom
of the fish and reptile. One morning last March,
I pressed against the new barbed and galvanized

fence on the Boston Common. Behind their cage,
yellow dinosaur steamshovels were grunting
as they cropped up tons of mush and grass
to gouge their underworld garage.

Parking spaces luxuriate like civic
sandpiles in the heart of Boston.
A girdle of orange, Puritan-pumpkin colored girders
braces the tingling Statehouse,

shaking over the excavations, as it faces Colonel Shaw
and his bell-cheeked Negro infantry
on St. Gaudens' shaking Civil War relief,
propped by a plank splint against the garage's earthquake.

Two months after marching through Boston,
half the regiment was dead;
at the dedication,
William James could almost hear the bronze Negroes breathe.

Their monument sticks like a fishbone
in the city's throat.
Its Colonel is as lean
as a compass-needle.

He has an angry wrenlike vigilance,
a greyhound's gentle tautness;
he seems to wince at pleasure,
and suffocate for privacy.

He is out of bounds now. He rejoices in man's lovely,
peculiar power to choose life and die—
when he leads his black soldiers to death,
he cannot bend his back.

On a thousand small town New England greens,
the old white churches hold their air
of sparse, sincere rebellion; frayed flags
quilt the graveyards of the Grand Army of the Republic.

The stone statues of the abstract Union Soldier
grow slimmer and younger each year—
wasp-wasted, they doze over muskets
and muse through their sideburns . . .

Shaw's father wanted no monument
except the ditch,
where his son's body was thrown
and lost with his 'niggers.'

The ditch is nearer.
There are no statues for the last war here;
on Boylston Street, a commercial photograph
shows Hiroshima boiling

over a Mosler Safe, the 'Rock of Ages'
that survived the blast. Space is nearer.
When I crouch to my television set,
the drained faces of Negro school-children rise like balloons.

Colonel Shaw
is riding on his bubble,
he waits
for the blesséd break.

The Aquarium is gone. Everywhere,
giant finned cars nose forward like fish;
a savage servility
slides by on grease.

from
NEAR THE OCEAN

Waking Early Sunday Morning

O to break loose, like the chinook
salmon jumping and falling back,
nosing up to the impossible
stone and bone-crushing waterfall—
raw-jawed, weak-fleshed there, stopped by ten
steps of the roaring ladder, and then
to clear the top on the last try,
alive enough to spawn and die.

Stop, back off. The salmon breaks
water, and now my body wakes
to feel the unpolluted joy
and criminal leisure of a boy—
no rainbow smashing a dry fly
in the white run is free as I,
here squatting like a dragon on
time's hoard before the day's begun!

Vermin run for their unstopped holes;
in some dark nook a fieldmouse rolls
a marble, hours on end, then stops;
the termite in the woodwork sleeps—
listen, the creatures of the night
obsessive, casual, sure of foot,
go on grinding, while the sun's
daily remorseful blackout dawns.

Fierce, fireless mind, running downhill.
Look up and see the harbor fill:
business as usual in eclipse
goes down to the sea in ships—
wake of refuse, dacron rope,

bound for Bermuda or Good Hope,
all bright before the morning watch
the wine-dark hulls of yawl and ketch.

I watch a glass of water wet
with a fine fuzz of icy sweat,
silvery colors touched with sky,
serene in their neutrality—
yet if I shift, or change my mood,
I see some object made of wood,
background behind it of brown grain,
to darken it, but not to stain.

O that the spirit could remain
tinged but untarnished by its strain!
Better dressed and stacking birch,
or lost with the Faithful at Church—
anywhere, but somewhere else!
And now the new electric bells,
clearly chiming, 'Faith of our fathers,'
and now the congregation gathers.

O Bible chopped and crucified
in hymns we hear but do not read,
none of the milder subtleties
of grace or art will sweeten these
stiff quatrains shovelled out four-square—
they sing of peace, and preach despair;
yet they gave darkness some control,
and left a loophole for the soul.

No, put old clothes on, and explore
the corners of the woodshed for
its dregs and dreck: tools with no handle,
ten candle-ends not worth a candle,

old lumber banished from the Temple,
damned by Paul's precept and example,
cast from the kingdom, banned in Israel,
the wordless sign, the tinkling cymbal.

When will we see Him face to face?
Each day, He shines through darker glass—
In this small town where everything
is known, I see His vanishing
emblems, His white spire and flag-
pole sticking out above the fog,
like old white china doorknobs, sad,
slight, useless things to calm the mad.

Hammering military splendor,
top-heavy Goliath in full armor—
little redemption in the mass
liquidations of their brass,
elephant and phalanx moving
with the times and still improving,
when that kingdom hit the crash:
a million foreskins stacked like trash . . .

Sing softer! But what if a new
diminuendo brings no true
tenderness, only restlessness,
excess, the hunger for success,
sanity of self-deception
fixed and kicked by reckless caution,
while we listen to the bells—
anywhere, but somewhere else!

O to break loose. All life's grandeur
is something with a girl in summer . . .
elated as the President

girdled by his establishment
this Sunday morning, free to chaff
his own thoughts with his bear-cuffed staff,
swimming nude, unbuttoned, sick
of his ghost-written rhetoric!

No weekends for the gods now. Wars
flicker, earth licks its open sores,
fresh breakage, fresh promotions, chance
assassinations, no advance.
Only man thinning out his kind
sounds through the Sabbath noon, the blind
swipe of the pruner and his knife
busy about the tree of life . . .

Pity the planet, all joy gone
from this sweet volcanic cone;
peace to our children when they fall
in small war on the heels of small
war—until the end of time
to police the earth, a ghost
orbiting forever lost
in our monotonous sublime.

Fourth of July in Maine
(FOR HARRIET WINSLOW)

Another summer! Our Independence
Day Parade, all innocence
of children's costumes, helps resist
the communist and socialist.
Five nations: Dutch, French, Englishmen,
Indians, and we, who held Castine,

rise from their graves in combat gear—
world-losers elsewhere, conquerors here!

Civil Rights clergy face again
the scions of the good old strain,
the poor who always must remain
poor and Republicans in Maine,
upholders of the American Dream,
who will not sink and cannot swim—
Emersonian self-reliance,
lethargy of Russian peasants!

High noon. Each child has won his blue,
red, yellow ribbon, and our statue,
a dandyish Union Soldier, sees
his fields reclaimed by views and spruce—
he seems a convert to old age,
small, callous, elbowed off the stage,
while the canned martial music fades
from scene and green—no more parades!

Blue twinges of mortality
remind us the theocracy
drove in its stakes here to command
the infinite, and gave this land
a ministry that would have made
short work of Christ, the Son of God,
and then exchanged His crucifix,
hardly our sign, for politics.

This white Colonial frame house,
willed downward, Dear, from you to us,
still matters—the Americas'
best artifact produced en masse.
The founders' faith was in decay,

and yet their building seems to say:
'Every time I take a breath,
my God you are the air I breathe.'

New England, everywhere I look,
old letters crumble from the Book,
China trade rubble, one more line
unravelling from the dark design
spun by God and Cotton Mather—
our *bel età dell' oro*, another
bright thing thinner than a cobweb,
caught in Calvinism's ebb.

Dear Cousin, life is much the same,
though only fossils know your name
here since you left this solitude,
gone, as the Christians say, for good.
Your house, still outwardly in form
lasts, though no emissary come
to watch the garden running down,
or photograph the propped-up barn.

If memory is genius, you
had Homer's, enough gossip to
repeople Trollope's Barchester,
nurses, Negro, diplomat, down-easter,
cousins kept up with, nipped, corrected,
kindly, majorfully directed,
though family furniture, décor,
and rooms redone meant almost more.

How often when the telephone
brought you to us from Washington,
we had to look around the room
to find the objects you would name-

lying there, ten years paralyzed,
half blind, no voice unrecognized,
not trusting in the afterlife,
teasing us for a carving knife.

High New England summer, warm
and fortified against the storm
by nightly nips you once adored,
though never going overboard,
Harriet, when you used to play
your chosen Nadia Boulanger
Monteverdi, Purcell, and Bach's
precursors on the Magnavox.

Blue-ribboned, blue-jeaned, named for you,
our daughter cartwheels on the blue—
may your proportion strengthen her
to live through the millennial year
Two Thousand, and like you possess
friends, independence, and a house,
herself God's plenty, mistress of
your tireless sedentary love.

Her two angora guinea pigs
are nibbling seed, the news, and twigs—
untroubled, petrified, atremble,
a mother and her daughter, so humble,
giving, idle and sensitive,
few animals will let them live,
and only a vegetarian God
could look on them and call them good.

Man's poorest cousins, harmonies
of lust and appetite and ease,
little pacific things, who graze

the grass about their box, they praise
whatever stupor gave them breath
to multiply before their death—
Evolution's snails, by birth,
outrunning man who runs the earth.

And now the frosted summer night-dew
brightens, the north wind rushes through
your ailing cedars, finds the gaps;
thumbtacks rattle from the white maps,
food's lost sight of, dinner waits,
in the cold oven, icy plates—
repeating and repeating, one
Joan Baez on the gramophone.

And here in your converted barn,
we burn our hands a moment, borne
by energies that never tire
of piling fuel on the fire;
monologue that will not hear,
logic turning its deaf ear,
wild spirits and old sores in league
with inexhaustible fatigue.

Far off that time of gentleness,
when man, still licensed to increase,
unfallen and unmated, heard
only the uncreated Word—
when God the Logos still had wit
to hide his bloody hands, and sit
in silence, while his peace was sung.
Then the universe was young.

We watch the logs fall. Fire once gone,
we're done for: we escape the sun,

rising and setting, a red coal,
until it cinders like the soul.
Great ash and sun of freedom, give
us this day the warmth to live,
and face the household fire. We turn
our backs, and feel the whiskey burn.

Central Park

Scaling small rocks, exhaling smog,
gasping at game-scents like a dog,
now light as pollen, now as white
and winded as a grounded kite—
I watched the lovers occupy
every inch of earth and sky:
one figure of geometry,
multiplied to infinity,
straps down, and sunning openly . . .
each precious, public, pubic tangle
an equilateral triangle,
lost in the park, half covered by
the shade of some low stone or tree.
The stain of fear and poverty
spread through each trapped anatomy,
and darkened every mote of dust.
All wished to leave this drying crust,
borne on the delicate wings of lust
like bees, and cast their fertile drop
into the overwhelming cup.

Drugged and humbled by the smell
of zoo-straw mixed with animal,
the lion prowled his slummy cell,

serving his life-term in jail—
glaring, grinding, on his heel,
with tingling step and testicle . . .
Behind a dripping rock, I found
a one-day kitten on the ground—
deprived, weak, ignorant and blind,
squeaking, tubular, left behind—
dying with its deserter's rich
Welfare lying out of reach:
milk cartons, kidney heaped to spoil,
two plates sheathed with silver foil.

Shadows had stained the afternoon;
high in an elm, a snagged balloon
wooed the attraction of the moon.
Scurrying from the mouth of night,
a single, fluttery, paper kite
grazed Cleopatra's Needle, and sailed
where the light of the sun had failed.
Then night, the night—the jungle hour,
the rich in his slit-windowed tower . . .
Old Pharaohs starving in your foxholes,
with painted banquets on the walls,
fists knotted in your captives' hair,
tyrants with little food to spare—
all your embalming left you mortal,
glazed, black, and hideously eternal,
all your plunder and gold leaf
only served to draw the thief . . .

We beg delinquents for our life.
Behind each bush, perhaps a knife;
each landscaped crag, each flowering shrub,
hides a policeman with a club.

Near the Ocean

(FOR E.H.L.)

The house is filled. The last heartthrob
thrills through her flesh. The hero stands,
stunned by the applauding hands,
and lifts her head to please the mob . . .
No, young and starry-eyed, the brother
and sister wait before their mother,
old iron-bruises, powder, 'Child,
these breasts . . .' He knows. And if she's killed

his treadmill heart will never rest—
his wet mouth pressed to some slack breast,
or shifting over on his back . . .
The severed radiance filters back,
athirst for nightlife—gorgon head,
fished up from the Aegean dead,
with all its stranded snakes uncoiled,
here beheaded and despoiled.

We hear the ocean. Older seas
and deserts give asylum, peace
to each abortion and mistake.
Lost in the Near Eastern dreck,
the tyrant and tryannicide
lie like the bridegroom and the bride;
the battering ram, abandoned, prone,
beside the apeman's phallic stone.

Betrayals! Was it the first night?
They stood against a black and white
inland New England backdrop. No dogs
there, horse or hunter, only frogs

chirring from the dark trees and swamps.
Elms watching like extinguished lamps.
Knee-high hedges of black sheep
encircling them at every step.

Some subway-green coldwater flat,
its walls tattooed with neon light,
then high delirious squalor, food
burned down with vodka . . . menstrual blood
caking the covers, when they woke
to the dry, childless Sunday walk,
saw cars on Brooklyn Bridge descend
through steel and coal dust to land's end.

Was it years later when they met,
and summer's coarse last-quarter drought
had dried the hardveined elms to bark—
lying like people out of work,
dead sober, cured, recovered, on
the downslope of some gritty green,
all access barred with broken glass;
and dehydration browned the grass?

Is it this shore? Their eyes worn white
as moons from hitting bottom? Night,
the sandfleas scissoring their feet,
the sandbed cooling to concrete,
one borrowed blanket, lights of cars
shining down at them like stars? . . .
Sand built the lost Atlantis . . . sand,
Atlantic ocean, condoms, sand.

Sleep, sleep. The ocean, grinding stones,
can only speak the present tense;
nothing will age, nothing will last,

or take corruption from the past.
A hand, your hand then! I'm afraid
to touch the crisp hair on your head—
Monster loved for what you are,
till time, that buries us, lay bare.

from
NOTEBOOK

1. *Harriet, born January 4, 1957*

Half a year, then a year and a half, then
ten and a half—the pathos of a child's fractions, turn-
ing up each summer. Her God a seaslug, God a queen
with forty servants, God—you gave up . . . things whirl
in the chainsaw bite of whatever squares
the universe by name and number. For
the hundredth time, we slice the fog, and round
the village with our headlights on the ground,
like the first philosopher Thales who thought all things water,
and fell in a well . . . trying to find a car
key. . . . It can't be here, and so it must be there
behind the next crook in the road or growth
of fog—there blinded by our feeble beams,
a face, clock-white, still friendly to the earth.

2. *Harriet*

A repeating fly, blueblack, thumbthick—so gross,
it seems apocalyptic in our house—
whams back and forth across the nursery bed
manned by a madhouse of stuffed animals,
not one a fighter. It is like a plane
dusting apple orchards or Arabs on the screen—
one of the mighty . . . one of the helpless. It
bumbles and bumps its brow on this and that,
making a short, unhealthy life the shorter.
I kill it, and another instant's added
to the horrifying mortmain of
ephemera: keys, drift, sea-urchin shells,
you packrat off with joy . . . a dead fly swept
under the carpet, wrinkling to fulfillment.

3. Elizabeth

An unaccustomed ripeness in the wood;
move but an inch and moldy splinters fall
in sawdust from the walls' aluminum-paint,
once loud and fresh, now aged to weathered wood.
Squalls of the seagull's exaggerated outcry
dim out in the fog. . . . *Pace, pace.* All day our words
were rusty fish-hooks—wormwood . . . Dear Heart's-Ease,
we rest from all discussion, drinking, smoking,
pills for high blood, three pairs of glasses—soaking
in the sweat of our hard-earned supremacy,
offering a child our leathery love. We're fifty,
and free! Young, tottering on the dizzying brink
of discretion once, you wanted nothing,
but to be old, do nothing, type and think.

4. Harriet

Spring moved to summer—the rude cold rain
hurries the ambitious, flowers and youth;
our flash-tones crackle for an hour, and then
we too follow nature, imperceptibly
change our mouse-brown to white lion's mane,
thin white fading to a freckled, knuckled skull,
bronzed by decay, by many, many suns . . .
Child of ten, three quarters animal,
three years from Juliet, half Juliet,
already ripened for the night on stage—
beautiful petals, what shall we hope for,
knowing one choice not two is all you're given,
health beyond the measure, dangerous
to yourself, more dangerous to others?

Searching

I look back to you, and cherish what I wanted:
your flashing superiority to failure,
hair of yellow oak leaves, the arrogant
tanned brunt in the snow-starch of a loosened shirt—
your bullying half erotic rollicking. . . .
The white bluffs rise above the old rock piers,
wrecked past insuring by two hurricanes.
As a boy I climbed those scattered blocks and left
the sultry Sunday seaside crowd behind,
seeking landsend, with my bending fishing rod
a small thread slighter than the dark arc of your eyebrow. . . .
Back at school, alone and wanting you,
I scratched my four initials, R.T.S.L.
like a dirty word across my bare, blond desk.

Hudson River Dream

I like trees, because I can never be at their eye-level;
not even when the stiff sash of the snowed-in farmhouse
slammed, as it always did, toward morning-rise;
I dreaming I was sailing a very small sailboat,
with my mother one-eighth Jewish, and *her* mother two-eighths,
down the Hudson, twice as wide as it is, wide as the Mississippi,
sliding under the pylons of the George Washington Bridge,
lacework groins as tall as twenty trees
(childhood's twice-as-wide and twice-as-high),
docking through the coalsmoke at a river café.
The Atlantic draws the river to no end. . . .
My knee-joints melted when I met you—
O why was I born of woman? Never to reach their eye-level,
seeing women's mouths while my date delays in the john.

First Love

Two grades above me, though two inches shorter,
Leon Straus, sixthgrade fullback, his reindeer shirt—
passion put a motor in my heart.
I pretended he lived in the house across the street.
In first love a choice is seldom and blinding:
acres of whitecaps strew that muddy swell,
old crap and white plastic jugs lodge on shore.
Later, we learn better places to cast
our saffron sperm, and grasp what wisdom fears,
breasts stacked like hawknests in her boyfriend's shirt,
thing a deft hand tips on its back with a stick. . . .
Is it refusal of error breaks our life—
the supreme artist, Flaubert, was a boy before
the mania for phrases enlarged his heart.

Walks

In those days no *casus belli* to fight the earth
for the familial, hidden fundamental—
on their walks they scoured the hills to find a girl,
tomorrow promised the courage to die content.
The willow stump put out thin wands in leaf,
green, fleeting flashes of unmerited joy;
the first garden, each morning . . . the first man—
birds laughing at us from the distant trees,
troubadours of laissez-faire and love.
Conservatives only want to have the earth,
the great beast clanking its chain of vertebrae. . . .
Am I a free man, if I have no servant?
If at the end of the long walk, my old dog dies of joy
when I sit down, a poor man at my fire?

Clytemnestra

'After my marriage, I found myself in constant
companionship with this almost stranger I found
neither agreeable, interesting, nor admirable,
though he was always kind and irresponsible.
The first years after our first child was born,
his daddy was out at sea; that helped, I could bask
on the couch of inspiration and my dreams.
Our courtship was rough, his disembarkation
unwisely abrupt. I was animal,
healthy, easily tired; I adored luxury,
and should have been an extrovert; I usually
managed to make myself pretty comfortable. . . .
Well,' she laughed, 'we both were glad to dazzle.
A genius temperament should be handled with care.'

Onionskin

It's fancy functional things love us best;
not butterfly useless or austere with use,
they touched my body to assume a body—
my half-pound silver ticker with two bopped lids,
whose splinter lever nicked my thumbnail, and set
time moving from six a.m. to six p.m.—
twice daily time stopped and its thin hands.
It goes a-begging, without me, it is lost.
Where is grandfather's old snakehead watchchain?
The onionskin typing paper I bought by mistake
in Bucksport Maine last August? The last sheet
creasing cuts my finger and seems to scream
as if *Fortuna* bled in the white wood
and felt the bloody gash that brought me life.

The March (1)
(FOR DWIGHT MACDONALD)

Under the too white marmoreal Lincoln Memorial,
the too tall marmoreal Washington Obelisk,
gazing into the too long reflecting pool,
the reddish trees, the withering autumn sky,
the remorseless, amplified harangues for peace—
lovely to lock arms, to march absurdly locked
(unlocking to keep my wet glasses from slipping)
to see the cigarette match quaking in my fingers,
then to step off like green Union Army recruits
for the first Bull Run, sped by photographers,
the notables, the girls . . . fear, glory, chaos, rout . . .
our green army staggered out on the miles-long green fields,
met by the other army, the Martian, the ape, the hero,
his new-fangled rifle, his green new steel helmet.

The March (2)

Where two or three were flung together, or fifty,
mostly white-haired, or bald, or women . . . sadly
unfit to follow their dream, I sat in the sunset
shade of our Bastille, the Pentagon,
nursing leg- and arch-cramps, my cowardly,
foolhardy heart; and heard, alas, more speeches,
though the words took heart now to show how weak
we were, and right. An MP sergeant kept
repeating, 'March slowly through them. Don't even brush
anyone sitting down.' They tiptoed through us
in single file, and then their second wave
trampled us flat and back. Health to those who held,
health to the green steel head . . . to your kind hands
that helped me stagger to my feet, and flee.

Ulysses

Shakespeare stand-ins, same string hair, gay, dirty . . .
there's a new poetry in the air, it's youth's
patent, lust coolly led on by innocence—
late-flowering Garden, far from Eden fallen,
and still fair! None chooses as his model
Ulysses landhugging from port to port for girls . . .
his marriage a cover for the underworld,
dark harbor of suctions and the second chance.
He won Nausicaa twenty years too late. . . .
Scarred husband and wife sit naked, one Greek smile,
thinking *we were bound to fall in love*
if only we stayed married long enough—
because our ships are burned and all friends lost.
How we wish we were friends with half our friends!

The Charles River (1)

The sycamores throw shadows on the Charles,
as the fagged insect splinters, drops and joins
the infinite that scatters loosening leaves,
the long-haired escort and his short-skirted girl.
The black stream curves as if it led a lover—
my blood is pounding; in workaday times,
I take cold comfort from its heart elation,
its endless handstand round the single I,
the pumping and thumping of my overfevered wish. . . .
For a week my heart has pointed elsewhere:
it brings us here tonight, and ties our hands—
if we leaned forward, and should dip a finger
into this river's momentary black flow,
infinite small stars would break like fish.

The Charles River (2)

The circuit of snow-topped rural roads, eight miles
to ten, might easily have been the world's top,
the North Pole, when I trailed on spreading skis
my guide, his unerring legs ten inches thick in wool,
and pinched my earlobes lest they turn to snowdrops—
hard knocks that school a lifetime; yet I went on swiping
small things. That knife, yellow-snow with eleven blades,
where is it? Somewhere, where it will outlast me,
though flawed already when I picked it up. . . .
And now, the big town river, once straight and dead as its
    highway,
shrinks to country river, bankscrub, dry ice,
a live muskrat muddying the moonlight. You trail me,
Woman, so small, if one could trust appearance,
I might be in trouble with the law.

Anne Dick (1), 1936

Father's letter to your father said
stiffly and much too tersely he'd been told
you visited my college rooms alone—
I can still crackle that slight note in my hand.
I see your pink father—you, the outraged daughter.
That morning nursing my dark, quiet fire
on the empty steps of the Harvard Fieldhouse in
vacation . . . saying the start of *Lycidas* to myself
fevering my mind and cooling my hot nerves—
we were nomad quicksilver and drove to Boston;
I knocked my father down. He sat on the carpet—
my mother calling from the top of the carpeted stairs,
their glass door locking behind me, no cover; you
idling in the station wagon, no retreat.

Anne Dick (2), 1936

Longer ago than I had lived till then . . .
before the *Anschluss*, the ten or twenty million
war-dead . . . but who knows now off-hand how many?
I wanted to marry you, we gazed through your narrow
bay window at the hideous concrete dome
of M.I.T., its last blanched, hectic glow
sunsetted on the bay of the Esplanade:
like the classical seaport done by Claude,
an artist more out of fashion now than Nero,
his heaven-vaulting aqueducts, swords forged from plowshares,
the fresh green knife of his unloved mother's death . . .
The blood of our spirit dries in veins of brickdust—
Christ lost, our only king without a sword,
turning the word *forgiveness* to a sword.

The Charles River (3)

No stars, only cars, the stars of man,
mount sky and highway; life is wild: ice straw
puts teeth in the shallows, the water smells and lives.
We walk a tightrope, this embankment, jewed—
no, yankeed—by highways down to a stubbly lip. . . .
Once—you weren't born then—an iron railing,
cheerless and dignified, policed this walk;
it matched the times, and had an esplanade,
stamping down grass and growth with square stone shoes;
a groan went up when the iron railing crashed. . . .
The Charles, half ink, half liquid coaldust,
bears witness to the health of industry—
wrong times, an evil dispensation; but who
can hope to enter heaven with clean hands?

The Charles River (4)

Seen by no visible eye, our night unbroken—
our motel bedroom is putty-gray and cold,
the shivering winds thrust through its concrete cube.
A car or two, then none; since midnight none.
Highways on three levels parallel the river,
roads patrol the river in her losing struggle,
a force of nature trying to breathe beneath
a jacket of lava. We lie parallel,
parallel to the river, parallel
to six roads—unhappy and awake,
awake and naked, like a line of Greeks,
facing a second line of Greeks—like them,
willing to enter the battle, and not come out . . .
morning's breathing traffic . . . its unbroken snore.

Harvard

I

The parochial school's green copper dome like
a green summer grove above the defoliated playground;
clouds puff in cotton wads on a low Dutch sky—
the top of the school resembles a Place des Vosges. . . .
Lying in bed, I see a blind white morning
rise to mid-heaven in a gaggle of snow—
a silk stocking is coiling on a wire hanger
rapier-bright . . . they dangle from my tree,
a long throw for a hard cold day . . . wind lifting
the stocking like the lecherous, lost leg. . . .
The students, my swarm-mates, rise in their hundreds, and
leave

the hive—they can keep time. I've slept so late,
I see my stubble whiten while I shave;
the stocking blows to smog, the steel coathanger stains.

II

We inch by the Boston waterfront on icepools,
carparks make the harbor invisible,
our relationship advances, then
declines to private jokes, the chaff of lust. . . .
Dark days, fair nights . . . yet they fell short—
in a studio near the Back Bay Station, the skylight
angular, night-bluish, blear and spinsterish—
both fighting off muscular cramps, the same fatigue. . . .
Yet tonight means something, something we
must let go willingly, and smash:
all flesh is grass, and like the flower of the grass—
nol lips, breasts, eyes, hands, lips, hair—
the overworked central heating bangs the frame,
as the milkhorse in childhood would clang the morning milk-
    can.

III

MORNING

The great dawn of Boston lifts from its black rag;
from Thanksgiving to Christmas, thick arctic snow
thawing to days of moderate, night-black balm—
I cannot sleep, my veins are mineral,
dirt-full as the arteries of a cracked white cup;
one wearies of looking expectantly for the worse—
Chaucer's old January made hay with May.
In this ever more enlightened bedroom,
I wake under the early rising sun,

sex indelible flowers on the air—
shouldn't I ask to hold to you forever,
body of a dolphin, breast of cloud?
You rival the renewal of the day,
clearing the puddles with your green sack of books.

In the Forties

By August, Brooklyn turned autumn, all
Prospect Pond could mirror. No sound; no talk;
dead matches nicked the water and expired
in target-circles of inverted sky,
nature's looking-glass . . . a little cold!
Our day was cold and short, love, and its sun
numb as the red carp, twenty inches long,
panting, a weak old dog, below a smashed
oar floating from the musty dock. . . . The fish
is fungus now; I wear a swollen face. . . .
I rowed for our reflection, but it slid
between my hands aground. There the squirrel,
a conservative and vegetarian,
keeps his roots and freehold, Love, unsliding.

1930's

'Nature never will betray us,' the poet swore,
choosing peeled staff, senility and psalter
to scrounge Northumberland for the infinite. . . .
We burned the sun of the universal bottle,
and summered on a shorefront—the dusk seal

nightly dog-paddling on the hawk for fish,
whiskering the giddy harbor, a black blanket
splotched with spangles of the sky, the sky—
and somewhere the Brook Trout dolphin by the housepiles,
grow common by mid-vacation as hamburger,
fish-translucence cooked to white of an egg. . . .
Summer vacations surround the college winter,
the reach of nature is longer than a car—
I am no bigger than the shoe I fit.

Picture in The Literary Life, a Scrapbook

A mag photo, before I was I, or my books—
a listener. . . . A cheekbone gumballs out my cheek;
too much live hair. My wife caught in that eye blazes,
an egg would boil in the tension of that hand,
my untied shoestrings write my name in the dust. . . .
I lean against the tree, and sharpen bromides
to serve our great taskmaster, the New Critic,
who loved the writing better than we ourselves. . . .
In those days, if I pressed an ear to the earth,
I heard the bass growl of Hiroshima.
In the *Scrapbook*, it's only the old die classics:
one foot in the grave, two fingers in their Life.
Who would rather be his indexed correspondents
than the boy Keats spitting out blood for time to breathe?

Blizzard in Cambridge

Risen from the blindness of teaching to bright snow,
everything mechanical stopped dead,

taxis no-fares . . . *the wheels grow hot from driving*—
ice-eyelashes, in my spring coat; the subway
too jammed and late to stop for passengers;
snow-trekking the mile from subway end to airport . . .
to all-flights-cancelled, fighting queues congealed
to telephones out of order, stamping buses,
rich, stranded New Yorkers staring with the wild, mild eyes
of steers at the foreign subway—then the train home,
jolting with stately grumbling: an hour in Providence,
in New Haven . . . the Bible. In darkness seeing
white arsenic numbers on the tail of a downed plane,
the smokestacks of abandoned fieldguns burning skyward.

Die Forelle

I lean on a bridgerail watching the clear calm,
a homeless sound of joy is in the sky:
a fisherman making falsecasts over a brook,
a two pound browntrout darting with scornful quickness,
drawing straight lines like arrows through the pool.
The man might as well snap his rod on his knee,
each shake of a boot or finger scares the fish;
trout will never hit flies in this brightness.
I go on watching, and the man keeps casting,
he wades, and stamps his feet, and muddies the water;
before I know it, his rod begins to dip.
He wades, he stamps, he shouts to turn the run
of the trout with his wetfly breathed into its belly—
broken whiplash in the gulp of joy.

Mexico

V

Midwinter in Cuernavaca, tall red flowers
stand up on many trees; the rock is in leaf.
Large wall-bricks like loaves of risen bread—
somewhere I must have met this feverish pink
and knew its message; or is it that I've walked
you past them twenty times, and now walk back?
The stream will not flow back to hand, not twice, not once.
I've waited, I think, a lifetime for this walk.
The white powder slides out beneath our feet,
the sterile white salt of purity and blinding:
your puffed lace blouse is salt. The red brick glides;
bread for a dinner never to be served. . . .
When you left, I thought of you each hour of the day,
each minute of the hour, each second of the minute.

VIII

Three pillows, end on end, rolled in a daybed
blanket—elastic, round, untroubled. For a second,
by some hallucination of my hand
I imagined I was unwrapping you. . . .
Two immovable nuns, out of habit, too fat to leave
the dormitory, have lived ten days on tea,
bouillon cubes and cookies brought from Boston.
You curl in your metal bunk-bed like my child,
I sprawl on an elbow troubled by the floor—
nuns packing, nuns ringing the circular iron stair,
nuns in pajamas scalloped through their wrappers,
nuns boiling bouillon, tea or cookies, nuns
brewing and blanketing reproval . . .
the soul groans and laughs at its lack of stature.

IX

Next to last day baking on the marble veranda,
the roasting brown rock, the smoking grass, the breath
of the world risen like the ripe smoke of chestnuts,
a cleavage dropping miles to the valley's body;
and the following sick and thoughtful day,
the red flower, the hills, the valley, the Volcano—
this not the greatest thing, though great; the hours
of shivering, ache and burning, when we charged
so far beyond our courage—altitude. . . .
No artist perhaps, you see the backs of phrases,
a girl too simple to lose herself in words—
I fall back in the end on honest speech;
infirmity's a food the flesh must swallow,
feeding our minds . . . the mind which is also flesh.

X

Poor Child, you were kissed so much you thought you were
    walked on;
yet you wait in my doorway with bluebells in your hair.
Those other me's, you think, are they meaningless in toto,
hills coarsely eyed for a later breathless conquest,
leaving no juice in the flaw, mind lodged in mind?
A girl's not quite mortal, she asks everything. . . .
If you want to make the frozen serpent dance,
you must sing it the music of its mouth:
Sleep wastes the day lifelong behind your eyes,
night shivers at noonday in the boughs of the fir. . . .
Our conversation moved from lust to love,
asking only coolness, stillness, conversation—
then days, days, days, days . . . how can I love you more,
short of turning into a criminal?

T. S. Eliot

Caught between two streams of traffic, in the gloom
of Memorial Hall and Harvard's war-dead. . . . And he:
'Don't you loathe to be compared with your relatives?
I do. I've just found two of mine reviewed by Poe.
He wiped the floor with them . . . and I was *delighted*.'
Then on with warden's pace across the Yard,
talking of Pound, 'It's balls to say he only
pretends to be Ezra. . . . He's better though. This year,
he no longer wants to rebuild the Temple at Jerusalem.
Yes, he's better. "*You* speak," he said, when he'd talked two
    hours.
By then I had absolutely nothing to *say*.'
Ah Tom, one muse, one music, had one your luck—
lost in the dark night of the brilliant talkers,
humor and honor from the everlasting dross!

Ezra Pound

Horizontal on a deckchair in the ward
of the criminal mad. . . . A man without shoestrings clawing
the Social Credit broadside from your table, you saying,
'. . . here with a black suit and black briefcase; in the brief,
an abomination, Possum's *hommage* to Milton.'
Then sprung; Rapallo, and the decade gone;
and three years later, Eliot dead, you saying,
'Who's left alive to understand my jokes?
My old Brother in the arts . . . besides, he was a smash of a
    poet.'
You showed me your blotched, bent hands, saying, 'Worms.
When I talked that nonsense about Jews on the Rome

wireless, Olga knew it was shit, and still loved me.'
And I, 'Who else has been in Purgatory?'
You, 'I began with a swelled head and end with swelled feet.'

End of a Year

These conquered kings pass furiously away;
gods die in flesh and spirit and live in print,
each library a misquoted tyrant's home.
A year runs out in the movies, must be written
in bad, straightforward, unscanning sentences—
stamped, trampled, branded on backs of carbons,
lines, words, letters nailed to letters, words, lines—
the typescript looks like a Rosetta Stone. . . .
One more annus mirabilis, its hero *hero demens*,
ill-starred of men and crossed by his fixed stars,
running his ship past sound-spar on the rocks. . . .
The slush-ice on the east bank of the Hudson
is rose-heather in the New Year sunset;
bright sky, bright sky, carbon scarred with ciphers.

New Year's Eve

By miracle, I left the party half
an hour behind you, reached home five hours drunker,
imagining I would live a million years,
a million quarts drunker than the gods of Jutland—
live through another life and two more wives.
Life is too short to silver over this tarnish.
The gods, employed to haunt and punish husbands,

have no hand for trigger-fine distinctions,
their myopia makes all error mortal. . . .
My Darling, prickly hedgehog of the hearth,
chocolates, cherries, hairshirt, pinks and glass—
when we joined in the sublime blindness of courtship,
loving lost all its vice with half its virtue.
Cards will never be dealt to us fairly again.

Words for Muffin, a Guinea-Pig

'Of late they leave the light on in my entry
so I won't scare, though I never scare in the dark;
I bless this arrow that flies from wall to window . . .
five years and a nightlight given me to breathe—
Heidegger said spare time is ecstasy. . . .
I am not scared, although my life was short;
my sickly breathing sounded like dry leather.
Mrs. Muffin! It clicks. I had my day.
You'll paint me like Cromwell with all my warts:
small mop with a tumor and eyes too popped for thought.
I was a rhinoceros when jumped by my sons.
I ate and bred, and then I only ate,
my life zenithed in the Lyndon Johnson 'sixties . . .
this short pound God threw on the scales, found wanting.'

The Restoration

The old king enters his study with the police;
it's much like mine left in my hands a month:
unopened letters, the thousand dead cigarettes,

open books, yogurt cups in the unmade bed—   .
the old king enters his study with the police,
but all in all his study is much worse than mine;
an edge of malice shows the thumb of man:
frames smashed, their honorary honours lost,
all his unopened letters have been answered.
He halts at woman-things that can't be his,
and says, 'To think that human beings did this!'
The sergeant picks up a defiled *White Goddess*,
or the old king's offprints on ideograms,
'Would a human beings do this things to these book?'

West Side Sabbath

(BREAKFAST)

WIFE, in her tower of *The New York Times*;
HUSBAND, rewriting his engagement book. . . .
WIFE: Nixon's in trouble. HUSBAND: Another family
brawl? WIFE: Nixon has profounder troubles.
HUSBAND: You mean our National Peace Offensive?
WIFE: *Entre autres*. HUSBAND: When Nixon weighs in,
does he outweigh *The New York Sunday Times*?
WIFE: Say that twice, and I'll fly to San Juan with Bruce . . .
Is our chance a monochrome Socialism,
Robespierre's gunpoint equality,
privilege slashed to a margin of survival?
Or the Student-Left's casually defined
anarchists' faith in playing the full deck—
who wants the monks without the fucking Maypole?

Stalin

Winds on the stems make them creak like things made by man;
a hedge of vines and bushes—three or four
kinds, grape-leaf, elephant-ear and alder,
an arabesque, imperfect and alive,
a hundred hues of green, the darkest shades
fall short of black, the whitest leaf-back short of white.
The state, if we could see behind the wall,
is woven of perishable vegetation.
Stalin? What shot him clawing up the tree of power—
millions plowed under with the crops they grew,
his intimates dying like the spider-bridegroom?
The large stomach could only chew success. What raised him
was an unusual lust to break the icon,
joke cruelly, seriously, and be himself.

Harpo Marx

Harpo Marx, your hands white-feathered the harp—
the only words you ever spoke were sound.
The movie's not always the sick man of the arts,
yours touched the stars; Harpo, your motion picture
is still life unchanging, not nature dead.
You dumbly memorized an unwritten script. . . .
I saw you first two years before you died,
a black-and-white fall, near Fifth in Central Park:
old blond hair too blonder, old eyes too young.
Movie trucks and five police trucks wheel to wheel
like covered wagons. The crowd as much or little.
I wish I had knelt. . . . I age to your wincing smile,
like Dante's movie, the great glistening wheel of life—
the genius *happy* . . . a generic actor.

Will Not Come Back
(VOLVERAN)

Dark swallows will doubtless come back killing
the injudicious nightflies with a clack of the beak;
but these that stopped full flight to see your beauty
and my good fortune . . . as if they knew our names—
they'll not come back. The thick lemony honeysuckle,
climbing from the earthroot to your window,
will open more beautiful blossoms to the evening;
but these . . . like dewdrops, trembling, shining, falling,
the tears of day—they'll not come back . . .
Some other love will sound his fireword for you
and wake your heart, perhaps, from its cool sleep;
but silent, absorbed, and on his knees,
as men adore God at the altar, as I love you—
don't blind yourself, you'll not be loved like that.

Reading Myself

Like thousands, I took just pride and more than just
struck matches that brought my blood to a boil;
I memorized the tricks to set the river on fire—
somehow never wrote something to go back to.
Can I suppose I am finished with wax flowers
and have earned my grass on the minor slopes of Parnassus. . . .
No honeycomb is built without a bee
adding a circle to circle, cell to cell,
the wax and honey of a mausoleum—
this round dome proves its maker is alive;
the corpse of the insect lives embalmed in honey,
prays that its perishable work live long
enough for the sweet-tooth bear to desecrate—
this open book . . . my open coffin.

For Ann Adden: Coda

I want you to see me when I have one head
again, not many, like a bunch of grapes.
The universe moves beneath me when I move,
a stream of heady, terrified poured stone. . . .
On my great days of sickness, I was God—
cry of blood for high blood that gives both tyrant
and tyrannized their short half-holiday. . . .
Now the earth is solid, the sky is light,
yet even on the steadiest day, dead noon,
I have to brace my hand against a wall
to keep myself from swaying—swaying wall,
straitjacket, hypodermic, helmeted
doctors, one crowd, white-smocked, in panic, hit,
and bury me running on the cleated field.

Dream, the Republican Convention

That night the mustard bush and goldenrod
and more unlikely yellows trod a spiral,
clasped in eviscerating blue china vases
like friendly snakes embracing—cool not cold. . . .
Brotherly, stacked and mean, the great Convention
throws out Americana like dead flowers:
choices, at best, that hurt and cannot cure;
many are chosen, and too few were called. . . .
And yet again, I see the yellow bush rise,
the golds of the goldenrod eclipse their vase—
each summer the young breasts escape the ribcage
a formation, I suppose, beyond the easel.
What can be is only what will be . . .
the sun warms the mortician, unpolluted.

Flaw
(FLYING TO CHICAGO)

My old eye-flaw sprouting bits and strings
gliding like dragon-kites in the Midwestern sky—
I am afraid to look closely, and count them;
today I am exhausted and afraid.
I look through the window at unbroken white cloud,
and see in it my many flaws are one,
a flaw with a tail the color of shed skin,
inaudible rattle of the rattler's disks.
God is design, even our ugliness
is the goodness of his will. It gives me warning,
the first scrape of the Thunderer's fingernail. . . .
Faust's soul-sale was perhaps to leave the earth,
yet death is sweeter, weariness almost lets
me taste its sweetness none will ever taste.

Publication Day

'Dear Robert: I wish you were not a complete stranger,
I wish I knew something more about your mercy,
could total your minimum capacity
for empathy—this varies so much from genius.
Can you fellow-suffer for a turned-down book?
Can you see through your tragic vision, and
have patience with one isolated heart?
Do you only suffer for other famous people,
and socially comforting non-entities?
Has the thistle of failure a place in your affection?
It's important to know these things; in your equestrian
portrait by Mailer, I don't find these things. . . .
I write as a woman flung from a sinking ship—
one raft in the distance . . . you represent that raft.'

Women, Children, Babies, Cows, Cats

'It was at My Lai or Sonmy or something,
it was this afternoon. . . . We had these orders,
we had all night to think about it—
we was to burn and kill, then there'd be nothing
standing, women, children, babies, cows, cats. . . .
As soon as we hopped the choppers, we started shooting.
I remember . . . as we was coming up upon one area
in Pinkville, a man with a gun . . . running—this lady . . .
Lieutenant LaGuerre said, "Shoot her." I said,
"You shoot her, I don't want to shoot no lady."
She had one foot in the door. . . . When I turned her,
there was this little one-month-year-old baby
I thought was her gun. It kind of cracked me up.'

Returning Turtle

Weeks hitting the road, one fasting in the bathtub,
raw hamburger mossing in the watery stoppage,
the room drenched with musk like kerosene—
no one shaved, and only the turtle washed.
He was so beautiful when we flipped him over:
greens, reds, yellows, fringe of the faded savage,
the last Sioux, old and worn, saying with weariness,
'Why doesn't the Great White Father put his red
children on wheels, and move us as he will?'
We drove to the Orland River, and watched the turtle
rush for water like rushing into marriage,
swimming in uncontaminated joy,
lovely the flies that fed that sleazy surface,
a turtle looking back at us, and blinking.

Growth (Harriet)

'I'm talking the whole idea of life, and boys,
with Mother; and then the heartache, when we're fifty. . . .
You've got to call your *Notebook, Book of the Century*,
but it will take you a century to write,
then I will have to revise it, when you die.'
Latin, Spanish, swimming half a mile,
writing a saga with a churl named Eric,
Spanish, Spanish, math and rollerskates;
a love of party dresses, but not boys;
composing something with the bells of *Boris:*
'UNTITLED, would have to be the name of it. . . .'
You grow apace, you grow too fast apace,
too soon adult; no, not adult, like us. . . .
On the telephone, they say, 'We're tired, aren't you?'

Seals

If we must live again, not us; we might
go into seals, we'd handle ourselves better:
able to dawdle, able to torpedo,
all too at home in our three elements,
ledge, water and heaven—if man could restrain his hand. . . .
We flipper the harbor, blots and patches and oilslick,
so much bluer than water, we think it sky.
Creature could face creator in this suit,
fishers of fish not men. Some other August,
the easy seal might say, 'I could not sleep
last night; suddenly I could write my name. . . .'
Then all seals, preternatural like us,
would take direction, head north—their haven
green ice in a greenland never grass.

Obit

Our love will not come back on fortune's wheel—

in the end it gets us, though a man know what he'd have:
old cars, old money, old undebased pre-Lyndon
silver, no copper rubbing through . . . old wives;
I could live such a too long time with mine.
In the end, every hypochondriac is his own prophet.
Before the final coming to rest, comes the rest
of all transcendence in a mode of being, hushing
all becoming. I'm for and with myself in my otherness,
in the eternal return of earth's fairer children,
the lily, the rose, the sun on brick at dusk,
the loved, the lover, and their fear of life,
their unconquered flux, insensate oneness, painful 'It was. . . .'
After loving you so much, can I forget
you for eternity, and have no other choice?

from
THE DOLPHIN

Fishnet

Any clear thing that blinds us with surprise,
your wandering silences and bright trouvailles,
dolphin let loose to catch the flashing fish. . . .
saying too little, then too much.
Poets die adolescents, their beat embalms them,
the archetypal voices sing offkey;
the old actor cannot read his friends,
and nevertheless he reads himself aloud,
genius hums the auditorium dead.
The line must terminate.
Yet my heart rises, I know I've gladdened a lifetime
knotting, undoing a fishnet of tarred rope;
the net will hang on the wall when the fish are eaten,
nailed like illegible bronze on the futureless future.

Symptoms

A dog seems to lap water from the pipes,
a wheeze of dogsmell and dogcompanionship—
life-enhancing water brims my bath—
(the bag of waters or the lake of the grave. . . . ?)
from the palms of my feet to my wet neck—
I have no mother to lift me in her arms.
I feel my old infection, it comes once yearly:
lowered good humor, then an ominous
rise of irritable enthusiasm. . . .
Three dolphins bear our little toilet-stand,
the grin of the eyes rebukes the scowl of the lips,
they are crazy with the thirst. I soak,
examining and then examining
what I really have against myself.

Voices

'What a record year, even for us—
last March, I knew you'd manage by yourself,
you were the true you; now finally
your clowning makes visitors want to call a taxi,
you tease the patients as if they were your friends,
your real friends who want to save your image
from this genteel, disgraceful hospital.
Your trousers are worn to a mirror. . . . That new creature.
when I hear her name, I have to laugh.
You left two houses and two thousand books,
a workbarn by the ocean, and two slaves
to kneel and wait upon you hand and foot—
tell us why in the name of Jesus.' Why
am I clinging here so foolishly alone?

Fall Weekend at Milgate

Milgate kept standing for four centuries,
good landlord alternating with derelict.
Most fell between. We're landlords for the weekend,
and watch October go balmy. Midday heat
draws poison from the Jacobean brick,
and invites the wilderness to our doorstep:
moles, nettles, last Sunday news, last summer's toys,
bread, cheeses, jars of honey, a felled elm
stacked like construction in the kitchen garden.
The warm day brings out wasps to share our luck,
suckers for sweets, pilots of evolution;
dozens drop in the beercans, clamber, buzz,
debating like us whether to stay and drown,
or, by losing legs and wings, take flight.

Mermaid

I

I have learned what I wanted from the mermaid
and her singeing conjunction of tail and grace.
Deficiency served her. What else could she do?
Failure keeps snapping up transcendence,
bubble and bullfrog boating on the surface,
belly lustily lagging three inches lowered—
the insatiable fiction of desire.
None swims with her and breathes the air.
A mermaid flattens soles and picks a trout,
knife and fork in chainsong at the spine,
weeps white rum undetectable from tears.
She kills more bottles than the ocean sinks,
and serves her winded lovers' bones in brine,
nibbled at recess in the marathon.

III

Our meetings are no longer like a screening;
I see the nose on my face is just a nose,
your *bel occhi grandi* are just eyes
in the photo of you arranged as figurehead
or mermaid on the prow of a Roman dory,
bright as the morning star or a blond starlet.
Our twin black and tin Ronson butane lighters
knock on the sheet, are what they are,
too many, and burned too many cigarettes. . . .
Night darkens without your necessary call,
it's time to turn your pictures to the wall;
your moon-eyes water and your nervous throat
gruffs my directive, '*You must go now go.*'
Contralto mermaid, and stone-deaf at will.

IV

I see you as a baby killer whale,
free to walk the seven seas for game,
warm-hearted with an undercoat of ice,
a nerve-wrung back . . . all muscle, youth, intention,
and skill expended on a lunge or puncture—
hoisted now from conquests and salt sea
to flipper-flapper in a public tank,
big deal for the Sunday ennui. . . . My blind love—
on the Via Veneto, a girl
counting windows in a glass café,
now frowning at her menu, now counting out
neanderthals flashed like shorebait on the walk. . . .
Your stamina as *inside-right* at school
spilled the topheavy boys, and keeps you pure.

V

One wondered who would see and date you next,
and grapple for the danger of your hand.
Will money drown you? Poverty, though now
in fashion, debases women as much as wealth.
You use no scent, dab brow and lash with shoeblack,
willing to face the world without more face.
I've searched the rough black ocean for you,
and saw the turbulence drop dead for you,
always lovely, even for those who had you,
Rough Slitherer in your grotto of haphazard.
I lack manhood to finish the fishing trip.
Glad to escape beguilement and the storm,
I thank the ocean that hides the fearful mermaid—
like God, I almost doubt if you exist.

Flounder

In a day we pass from the northern lights
to doomsday dawns. Crowds crush to work at eight,
and walk with less cohesion than the mist;
the sky, without malice, is acid, Christmas lights
are needed to reveal the Thames. God sees—
wash me as white as the sole I ate last night,
acres of whiteness, back of Folkestone sand,
cooked and skinned and white—the heart appeased.
Soles live in depth, see not, spend not . . . eat;
their souls are camouflaged to die in dishes,
flat on their backs, the posture of forgiveness—
squinch-eyes, bubbles of bloodshot worldliness,
unable ever to turn the other cheek—
at sea, they bite like fleas whatever we toss.

Exorcism

This morning, as if I were home in Boston, snow,
the pure witchery-bitchery of kindergarten winters;
my window whitens like a movie screen,
glaring, specked, excluding rival outlook—
I can throw what I want on this blank screen,
but only the show already chosen shows:
Melodrama with her stiletto heel
dancing bullet wounds in the parquet
My words are English, but the plot is hexed:
one man, two women, the common novel plot.
what you love you are. . . .
You can't carry your talent with you like a suitcase.
Don't you dare mail us the love your life denies;
do you really know *what you have done?*

Plotted

Planes are like arrows through the highest sky,
ducks V the ducklings across a puckered pond;
Providence turns animals to things.
I roam from bookstore to bookstore browsing books,
I too maneuvered on a guiding string
as I execute my written plot.
I feel how Hamlet, stuck with the Revenge Play
his father wrote him, went scatological
under this clotted London sky.
Catlike on a paper parapet,
he declaimed the words his prompter fed him,
knowing convention called him forth to murder,
loss of free will and licence of the stage.
Death's not an event in life, it's not lived through.

Artist's Model

'If it were done, twere well it were done quickly—
to quote a bromide, your vacillation
is acne.' And we totter off the strewn stage,
knowing tomorrow's migraine will remind us
how drink heightened the brutal flow of elocution. . . .
We follow our plot obediently as actors,
divorced from making a choice by our vocation.
'If you woke and found an egg in your shoe,
would you feel you'd lost this argument?'
It's over, my clothes fly into your borrowed suitcase,
the good day is gone, the broken champagne glass
crashes in the ashcan . . . private whims, and illusions,
too messy for our character to survive.
I come on walking off-stage backwards.

Mermaid Emerging

The institutions of society
seldom look at a particular—
Degas's snubnosed dancer swings on high,
legging the toplights, never leaving the stage,
enchanting lovers of art, discerning none.
Law fit for all fits no one like a glove. . . .
Mermaid, why are you another species?
'Because, you, I, everyone is unique.'
Does anyone ever make you do anything?
'Do this, do that, do nothing; you're not chained.
I am a woman or I am a dolphin,
the only animal man really loves,
I spout the smarting waters of joy in your face—
rough weather fish, who cuts your nets and chains.'

Angling

Withdrawn to a third your size, and frowning doubts,
you stare in silence through the afterdinner,
when wine takes our liberty and loosens tongues—
fair-face, ball-eyes, profile of a child,
except your eyelashes are always blacked,
each hair colored and quickened like tying a fly.
If a word amuses you, the room includes your voice,
you are audible; none can catch you out,
your flights are covered by a laughing croak—
a flowered dress lost in the flowered wall.
I am waiting like an angler with practice and courage;
the time to cast is now, and the mouth open,
the huge smile, head and shoulders of the dolphin—
I am swallowed up alive . . . I am.

Late Summer at Milgate

A sweetish smell of shavings, wax and oil
blows through the redone bedroom newly aged;
the sun in heaven enflames a sanded floor.
Age is our reconciliation with dullness,
my varnish complaining, *I will never die.*
I still remember more things than I forgo:
once it was the equivalent of everlasting
to stay loyal to my other person loved—
in the fallen apple lurked a breath of spirits,
the uninhabitable granite shone
in Maine, each rock our common gravestone. . . .
I sit with my staring wife, children . . . the dour Kent sky
a smudge of mushroom. In temperate years the grass
stays green through New Year—I, my wife, our children.

Robert Sheridan Lowell

Your midnight ambulances, the first knife-saw
of the child, feet-first, a string of tobacco tied
to your throat that won't go down, your window heaped
with brown paper bags leaking peaches and avocados,
your meals tasting like Kleenex . . . too much blood is seep-
        ing . . .
after twelve hours of labor to come out right,
in less than thirty second swimming the blood-flood:
Little Gingersnap Man, homoform,
flat and sore and alcoholic red,
only like us in owning to middle-age.
'If you touch him, he'll burn your fingers.'
'It's his health, not fever. Why are the other babies so pallid?

His navy-blue eyes tip with his head. . . . Darling,
we have escaped our death-struggle with our lives.'

Careless Night

So country-alone, and O so very friendly,
our heaviness lifted from us by the night . . .
we dance out into its diamond suburbia,
and see the hill-crown's unrestricted lights—
all day these encroaching neighbours are out of sight.
Huge smudge sheep in burden becloud the grass,
they swell on moonlight and weigh two hundred pounds—
hulky as you in your white sheep-coat, as nervous to gallop. . . .
The Christ-Child's drifter shepherds have left this field,
gone the shepherd's breezy too predictable pipe.
Nothing's out of earshot in this daylong night;
nothing can be human without man.
What is worse than hearing the late-born child crying—
and each morning waking up glad we wake?

Wildrose

A mongrel image for all summer, our scene at breakfast:
a bent iron fence of straggly wildrose glowing
below the sausage-rolls of new-mown hay—
Sheridan splashing in his blue balloon tire:
whatever he touches he's told not to touch
and whatever he reaches tips over on him.
Things have gone on and changed, the next oldest
daughter bleaching her hair three shades lighter with beer—
but if you're not a blonde, it doesn't work. . . .

Sleeping, the always finding you there with day,
the endless days revising our revisions—
everyone's wildrose? . . . And our golden summer
as much as such people can. When most happiest
how do I know I can keep any of us alive?

Lost Fish

My heavy step is treacherous in the shallows—
once squinting in the sugared eelgrass for game,
I saw the glass torpedo of a big fish,
power strayed from unilluminating depth,
roaming through the shallows worn to bone.
I was seven, and fished without a hook.
Luckily, Mother was still omnipotent—
a battered sky, a more denuded lake,
my heavy rapier trolling rod bent *L*,
drowned stumps, muskrat huts, my record fish,
its endless waddling outpull like a turtle. . . .
The line snapped, or my knots pulled—I am free
to reach the end of the marriage on my knees.
The mud we stirred sinks in the lap of plenty.

Sick

I wake now to find myself this long alone,
the sun struggling to renounce ascendancy—
two elephants are hauling at my head.
It might have been redemptive not to have lived—

in sickness, mind and body might make a marriage
if by depression I might find perspective—
a patient almost earns the beautiful,
a castle, two cars, old polished heirloom servants,
Alka Seltzer on his breakfast tray—
the fish for the table bunching in the fishpond.
None of us can or wants to tell the truth,
pay fees for the over-limit we caught, while floating
the lonely river to senility
to the open ending. Sometimes in sickness,
we are weak enough to enter heaven.

On the End of the Phone

My sidestepping and obliquities, unable
to take the obvious truth on any subject—
why do I do what I do not want to say?
When everything matters, ask and never know?
Your rapier voice—I have had so much—
hundred words a minute, piercing and thrilling . . .
the invincible lifedrive of everything alive,
ringing down silver dollars with each word. . . .
Love wasn't what went wrong, we kept our daughter;
what a good father is is no man's boast—
to be still friends when we're no longer children. . . .
Why am I talking from the top of my mouth?
I am talking to you transatlantic,
we're almost talking in one another's arms.

Dolphin

My Dolphin, you only guide me by surprise,
a captive as Racine, the man of craft,
drawn through his maze of iron composition
by the incomparable wandering voice of Phèdre.
When I was troubled in mind, you made for my body
caught in its hangman's-knot of sinking lines,
the glassy bowing and scraping of my will. . . .
I have sat and listened to too many
words of the collaborating muse,
and plotted perhaps too freely with my life,
not avoiding injury to others,
not avoiding injury to myself—
to ask compassion . . . this book, half fiction,
an eelnet made by man for the eel fighting—

my eyes have seen what my hand did.

Notes

In a valuable appendix to his book, *Robert Lowell: the First Twenty Years*, Hugh B. Staples has closely annotated many of Lowell's early poems. Readers in search of more detailed information about Lowell's sources and references are advised to consult Staples. I have drawn freely on Staples's detective work.

Page 37   *'The Holy Innocents'*

A tense, difficult poem in which Lowell characteristically enforces a shock encounter between the past and present. The landscapes of biblical Israel and wartime New England have been mysteriously merged. As Herod slaughtered the Holy Innocents in a vain attempt to destroy the infant Christ, so in 1944 ('The nineteen-hundred forty-fifth of grace') the world was smoking under the bombs and military campaigns of both the Allies and the Axis powers. The ancient oxen, straying from some Christmas crib, and the modern automobiles are seen to be climbing the same hill in New Hampshire. Finally, in a characteristically bold Lowellian gesture, the blundering innocence of the oxen is compared to the innocence of Jesus Himself. Does the Child 'lie still' in the last line of the poem because of His divine tranquillity, or because the riven world of 1944 has proved too much for Him? Lowell seems here to be testing his own faith, painfully submitting to the proposition that God is dead. The 'clinkered hill of our purgation' has already taken nearly two thousand years to climb; how much longer can it take for the world to be purged of its accumulated burden of sin? The questions are anguished, and they breed a poetic style which is knotty with paradoxes and harsh juxtapositions. Yet the rhyme scheme is subtle and tesselated, looping its way intricately through the poem; and the metre has a striking argumentative rigidity. In many of these early poems, Lowell uses a loping iambic pentameter in which he jogs along, putting in irregular stresses just often enough to keep the pace fluid and unforced. So here lines 1, 2, 8, 14, and the final line of the poem are opened by a word with an irregular, strong stress on its initial syllable; and these controlled breaks with an otherwise strict pattern give Lowell the bite and grittiness of tone which marks his style at this period. *Ale-wife run*. The ale-wife is a small minnowy fish, common in New England; it lives in the sea and spawns in fresh water.

Lowell now wishes to see this poem printed by itself; previously it has always appeared as Section VI of 'The Quaker Graveyard in Nantucket', as the invocation of the drowning sailor in line 9 reminds us. Walsingham is a Norfolk village with both Catholic and Anglican shrines commemorating Richeldes of Faveraches's vision of the Virgin Mary. Most of Lowell's poem is a verse-adaptation of a prose passage in E. I. Watkin's *Catholic Art and Culture*; and Lowell himself had never been to Walsingham. Yet what in Watkin is a straightforward description of the landscape and the statue of the Virgin turns in Lowell's hands into another highly personal exploration of his own eccentric, fundamentally humanist theology. For Watkin, the statue is unremarkable, without charm or comeliness, 'expressionless'. For Lowell, these impersonal qualities are profoundly expressive of the essential paradox of Christian faith. The barefooted pilgrims, or Warren Winslow, Lowell's cousin drowned in the north Atlantic, come to seek spiritual succour from the dispassionate, inscrutable figure at the centre of the shrine. Will she, like the still Child in 'The Holy Innocents', be strong enough to intercede for a century so far gone in its troubles? Here, as elsewhere, Lowell is deeply concerned with the nature of divine grace; it seems, indeed, to be the very paradox of grace—the incongruous, impartial stillness of both the Virgin and the infant Christ—which is its strength, and both of these poems almost take the form of prayers for a miracle. There is nothing pious or smug in Lowell's religion; both poems are taut with the difficulty and improbability of faith. Yet: 'the world shall come to Walsingham', and the force of that line, won in the poem against long odds, is a measure of the vigour of Lowell's religious imagination.

Page 38   'The Quaker Graveyard in Nantucket'

Lowell, dissatisfied with the sprawl of this poem in its previously printed form, has cut it down drastically for this edition; as it is printed here it has an expressionistic concision, rapid, allusive and oblique. The island of Nantucket, lying south of Cape Cod off the eastern seaboard, was the centre of the whaling industry in the nineteenth century. In *Moby Dick* Melville wrote:

> The Nantucketer, he alone resides and riots on the sea; he alone, in Bible language, goes down to it in ships; to and fro ploughing it as his own special plantation. *There* is his home; *there* lies his business, which a Noah's flood would not interrupt, though it

overwhelmed all the millions in China. He lives on the sea, as prairie cocks on the prairie; he hides among the waves, he climbs them as chamois hunters climb the Alps.

Lowell's elegy for his cousin interweaves strands of biblical, classical and New England marine mythology. It starts with an adaptation of a prose description of a shipwreck by Melville's contemporary, H. D. Thoreau (from *Cape Cod*), then moves on to *Moby Dick* and Captain Ahab's heroic, self-destructive pursuit of the white whale, through the myths of Orpheus in the underworld and Odysseus and the Sirens, and ends with Jonah as a pre-Christian version of the resurrected Messiah. Notice how the poem begins with death, with the burial at sea of the drowned sailor, and ends, paradoxically, with the divine Creation, with God fashioning 'man from sea's slime'. It is yet another poem about a miracle; its subject is nothing less than the nature of salvation.

For Lowell, as for Melville, the mariner at sea is engaged on a fatal quest—that search for knowledge which makes him parallel and re-enact Adam's first sin. After the shipwreck we see the sailors in a state of prelapsarian innocence; the Quakers died, Lowell says, 'When time was open-eyed/ Wooden and childish'. But in the third section of the poem, as the harpoon tears into the flukes of the whale, a vision of a fallen world dramatically opens up: 'When the whale's viscera go and the roll/ Of its corruption shall overrun this world. . . .' Like Milton, Lowell seems to enjoy himself most when he is writing about sin, and this section is rich and sensual in its contemplation of a released and flooding evil. Only prayer and grace can save: Jonah, the sailors' patron who, like Christ, died and was symbolically born again when he emerged from the belly of the whale, is called on by the sinners who are drowning in an ocean of corruption that they themselves have let loose. The poem ends with a redemption both glorious and inexplicable: the rainbow of the Lord's will is beyond human understanding, beyond the realm of the poem.

Yet although 'The Quaker Graveyard in Nantucket' is a terse and powerful theological statement, its Atlantic Ocean is a very real sea; the site of a real and barbarous naval war. We are never far from the guns and the 'steeled fleet' of Warren Winslow's twentieth-century Atlantic, and much of the force of the poem derives from Lowell's horror at the meaningless destruction of war. Yet again, Lowell shows us a world so far gone in human corruption that even God might seem powerless to save it. Yet again, he presents us with a divinity who betrays not a flicker of compassion. He demands from the reader an uncompromising faith in miracles.

Page 41   '*The Drunken Fisherman*'

This poem too has been pared down by Lowell for this edition. Based on Christ's promise to the Apostles, 'I will make you fishers of men . . .', it is a brilliant dramatic monologue. Angling has always been an important source of poetic images for Lowell; the encounter between man and fish, the hunter and the hunted, the human and the animal, recurs again and again in his work. The hero of *The Dolphin* fishes for the woman he loves across a restaurant table; and throughout the book she is conceived as having the elusive, impenetrable intelligence and beauty of an aquatic creature—a dolphin, a fish, a mermaid. In 'The Drunken Fisherman' we glimpse Melville's Ahab chasing Moby Dick, and again the New England whaling industry is seen to be possessed of an Edenic innocence. 'Once fishing was a rabbit's foot. . . .' The water in which Lowell's modern fisherman stands is bloody and dynamited; like the twentieth century itself, it reeks of carnage. And the fisherman himself is crazed and unwilling, a drunken, reluctant disciple. The river he fishes turns out, at the end of the poem, to be his own bloodstream; so is the 'bloody sty' man's body? Is the speaker of the poem really the soul of man, nauseated by its corporeal cage?

Page 42   '*Between the Porch and the Altar*'

From the Ash Wednesday epistle, taken from the Book of Joel: 'Between the porch and the altar, the priests, the Lord's ministers, shall weep, and shall say: Spare, O Lord, Spare Thy people.' In Lowell's poem Man shrives himself in confession as he relives his relationships with his mother, his mistress, and his wife. At the end of the poem, the priest recites a funeral mass over the coffin of Man at the Day of Judgement, while Man, reduced again to infancy in the 'baby-carriage' of the coffin, is rocked by the hand of a vengeful God of Fire.

At the same time, the poem is a savage epitaph on the history of New England. The setting is Concord, where the 'Farmer' who 'sizzles on his shaft all day' is the statue of the Concord Minute-Man. (The Minute-Men were scratch guerrillas raised in New England townships during the war of independence; Lowell frequently— to the considerable alarm of many American historians—treats the Minutemen as archetypal freedom-fighters. Their actual behaviour is reputed to have been somewhat inglorious.) Here the freedom which the American colonists wrested from their English masters is equated with the Christian doctrine of the freedom of the will. In 'Between the Porch and the Altar' we are presented with a vision of an America gone rankly to seed, a corrupted garden. In it nature is savage: represented by a snake swallowing a duckling, a bitter New England winter, and a landscape peopled with serpents. The human beings in the poem have a nightmare sharpness: the mother in the first section is an obscene effigy; Adam and Eve turn into serpents themselves when they embrace; the mistress, Katherine, is in the throes of mania; and Man himself is finally humbled in death, a squalling child once more. Thus, Lowell implies, has free will been misused. One wants to note yet again that Lowell's religion stops short of consolation; his Christianity seems merely to intensify his vision of a fecund corruption.

This poem is stylistically important in Lowell's development as a writer. For the first time we are exposed to the full force of that unique poetic doggerel which is able to catch the pace and the manic leaps of association of a sensibility in flood. The finest parts of 'Between the Porch and the Altar' are charged, as the poetry of Yeats is charged, with an urgent, often confused, irrationality. The hectic proliferation of symbols, objects, images, intuitions proceeds faster than logic—one important reason why Lowell's poetry so often proves to be an explicator's graveyard.

Page 46   *'At the Indian Killer's Grave'*

From the churchyard of King's Chapel, Boston, where some of Lowell's own ancestors are buried—another garden that has gone rotten—Lowell grimly contemplates the seamy underside of New England history, from the Indian massacres of the Puritans to the 'Easter crowds' of the modern Boston-Irish. Subways run through the soil where the dead lie; there are 'frayed cables' on the family cenotaph of the Winslows; and the 'dusty leaves and frizzled lilacs' suggest that nature itself has become exhausted. It was Marvell who said, 'The grave's a fine and private place . . .', but this modern, desolated graveyard is no longer even private. In the third stanza of the poem, Lowell shows us the dead merely descending into the subway cut beneath the chapel, or into the network of subterranean city drains. It all seems an impossible distance from the Garden of the final stanza, where the poet, longing for his own death, is received by the Virgin. The image with which the poem ends is extraordinary: theologically eccentric, sensual to the point of being erotic. If the 'sudden Bridegroom' is Christ, then he is both the Virgin's child, contained in her womb, and her lover, penetrating the 'trellis' in symbolic intercourse. Or is the Bridegroom the poet, wooing the Virgin, redeemed in death?

Such juxtapositions of the physical and the spiritual, often deliberately shocking at first sight, are characteristic of devotional verse. The seventeenth-century American metaphysical poet Edward Taylor, for instance, speaks of 'God's Tender Bowells run/ Out streams of Grace. . . .' In our fallen world sexuality and excretion are low functions of the body; in a world of divine grace they transcend their human associations. Both Lowell and Edwards are fond of shocking the reader into faith; they present us with paradoxes that only faith and grace can reconcile. Their very implausibility becomes a celebration of the miracle of the divine order.

Page 48   'In the Cage'

Lowell spent a five-month term in Federal Prison in 1943–4, after his plea of conscientious objection had been turned down by the court. In interview, Lowell has said: 'Jail was monotonous and weak on incident. I queued for hours for cigarettes and chocolate bars, and did slow make-work like wheeling wheelbarrows full of cinders. I found life lulling. I slept amongst eighty men, a foot apart, and grew congenial with other idealist felons, who took home-made stands. I was thankful to find jail gentler than boarding school or college—an adult fraternity. I read—*Erewhon* and *The Way of all Flesh* . . . and God knows what now . . . two thousand pages of Proust. I left jail educated—not as they wished *re*-educated.'

In the poem, prison is seen as a coal-mine, or a hell. The canaries beating their bars are the canaries that miners used to take down the pit to detect dangerous escapes of gas. The two fellow prisoners who are observed in detail by Lowell are both blacks—because they look like miners covered in coaldust, or because black is the colour of Adam's original sin? The twin colours of this poem—black and yellow—reverberate elsewhere in Lowell's work; see, for instance, 'The Drinker', p. *88*.

Page 48   'Mr. Edwards and the Spider'

Jonathan Edwards (1703–58) was a great American Calvinist divine. At the age of thirteen he wrote an essay about 'the flying spider', and in 1741 he returned to the insect when he preached his most famous sermon, 'Sinners in the Hands of an Angry God'. 'The God that holds you over the pit of hell, much as one holds a spider or some loathsome insect over the fire, abhors you, and is dreadfully provoked. . . . You hang by a slender thread, with the flames of divine wrath flashing about it. . . .' Lowell's poem adapts Edwards's own words. Josiah Hawley, the man threatened in the last stanza, was Edwards's uncle. He committed suicide.

This poem is a spectacular example of Lowell's ability to stage a continuing dialogue with the writers of the past. Edwards's eighteenth-century Calvinism is assimilated into Lowell's twentieth-century Catholicism. Yet perhaps the nature of death, as humans fear and contemplate it, has changed in those two hundred years. Why, in the last line, is death the 'Black Widow'? It is, of course, so named from the poisonous spider, and death itself widows. Yet Lowell's phrase seems to carry a further implication: that death *is* a widow—in the twentieth century it has lost the consolation of the promise of an afterlife as it has lost the logic of a divine judgement. For Edwards, death signifies the abundant grace, justice and order of a living, if vengeful, God; for Lowell, it has the arbitrariness of the bite of a spider. From a widowed death we have even more to fear, no God to count the minutes by the trillion.

Page 53   *'Beyond the Alps'*
On a train journey from Rome to Paris, Lowell makes a journey through time as he traverses space. The Europe of 1950 is interwoven with the classical cultures of Greece and Rome. The 'City of God' in line 8 is both Rome itself, home of the Vatican, and Saint Augustine's book of that title. The ambiguity is characteristic of the poem: thus the Swiss Everest expedition turn into the 'costumed Switzers' of the Hapsburg empire. The 'skirt-mad Mussolini' and Pope Pius XII with his buzzing electric razor are set against Rome under Caesar and the great age of the Latin satirists. Yet in this poem the past is made to sound as bad and murderous as the present: were the ravages of the Greek and Roman empires any less terrible than the ruinous state of post-world-war Europe? And, just as Caesar carved up Europe on his expeditions, so the satirists 'tore the tits/ and bowels of the Mother Wolf to bits'. The poem breeds images of carnivorous mutilation and has a tone of sickened violence. It arrives at a horrific analogue for our own time in the figure of Minerva.

For Minerva was the goddess of both the arts and war, and Lowell clearly means us to take the implication that literature thrives on destruction. What is bad for man is history—the greed and carnage of empire—may be meat for the poet. Later in Lowell's work, especially in *Notebook*, this life-in-death paradox becomes a central concern, and the poet is often observed feeding from the carrion of his own dead flesh. Is the Pope with his razor and canary an augur of a new, more lethargic and evasive world? Is there an implicit connexion between the canary of this poem and the 'yellow chirper' of Fear in 'In the Cage'?

The 'killer kings on an Etruscan cup' are the black-figure paintings on the vases which the Etruscans buried with their dead in ceremonial tombs. Great battles and scenes from mythology were recorded in a frieze around the body of the vase; and the black paint was subsequently scored with an awl to reveal details. Thus the description of Paris as 'our black classic' refers to its actual colour, as well as to its moral qualities. Why is Paris seen as breaking up? This may be a reference to the Etruscan cup, as it crumbles with age—a suggestion, perhaps, that not even the most funereal art survives. Paris, the city, centre of nineteenth- and early twentieth-century culture, is doomed, in Lowell's image, to become a decadent relic of a past that will seem as distant as the derivative art of the Etruscans.

Page 55　　　　'*Inauguration Day: January 1953*'

A grim, satiric commemoration of the inauguration of Dwight Eisenhower when he succeeded to the presidency of the United States in 1953. The statue of Peter Stuyvesant, the founder of New York, is symbolically buried under the snow for the occasion. Manhattan Island, the centre of New York's social and commercial life, is seen 'trussed' between the subways beneath it and the 'El', or elevated railway, overhead; in Lowell's poem, New York has become degenerate and corpulent. Cold Harbour was Grant's Pyrrhic victory over Lee at the end of the Civil War. Ulysses Grant, commander of the Union forces during the Civil War, was, like Eisenhower, a military general who later became a (notoriously bad) president. His statue, too, is lifeless; his sword permanently fixed in its groove. Possibly Lowell here intends to echo Yeats's famous coda to 'Under Ben Bulben':

> *Cast a cold eye*
> *On life, on death.*
> *Horseman, pass by!*

But Lowell's horseman is an immobile equestrian statue. Indeed, even the stars have a lifeless fixity: the national flag—the 'stars-and-stripes' —renders them identical and equidistant. Is the mausoleum in the Republic's heart all that is left to America: a brave past preserved only in statues and flags?

Page 55   '*A Mad Negro Soldier Confined at Munich*'
See Introduction, p. *22*. A dramatic monologue in which Lowell comes closer to Browning than anywhere else in his work, taking on the mask of an extreme and alien character and speaking through it. Blacks recur in his work as powerful and subversive figures (compare this poem with 'In the Cage', for instance). Lowell seems to have absorbed much of the southern mythology of the Negro; they are part of the underside of American history, and there is a suggestion in Lowell, as in the novels of William Faulkner, that the black is a perpetual reminder to the white of his own original sin. There is a strong Manichean strain in Lowell's imagination (the heresy of the Manichees lay basically in their belief that the world was a battleground for the equally matched forces of darkness and light), and his Negroes are prone to display the mark of Cain.

Page 56   '*My Last Afternoon with Uncle Devereux Winslow*'
(See also Introduction, p. *24*.) This brilliant family portrait has the seeming-ease of relaxed conversation and the social density and directness of prose fiction. As I have tried to demonstrate in the Introduction, its prosody and metrical structure are more subtle, more elaborate, more planned, than a quick reading of the poem initially suggests. He has opened up his poetic line so that it can take in everything from family gossip to elaborate classical parallels. What, for instance, does one make of the two lines in the final section:

> unseen and all-seeing, I was Agrippina
> in the Golden House of Nero. . . .

Agrippina was Nero's mother and she ruled for him at the beginning of his reign (Nero acceded to the emperorship at seventeen). Later, Nero gave orders that she was to be assassinated. The parallel between Lowell the child and Agrippina the emperor's mother seems, to begin with, a bit far-fetched. Yet it is full of a concentrated logic. The child in his grandfather's house discovers signs everywhere of these remote grownups' own childhoods. And in these signs, he comes upon the shadow of his own mortality. Queen of his own life for a short season, he, like Agrippina, is going to die too. The piles of lime, capable of breaking down corpses, become his own premature, imagined grave. The poem itself turns into a treasure trove of valued family history, of dated references and details, of old scandals and gossip—a treasure trove stored up against the death and dissolution of the family itself.

Page 61   'Commander Lowell' 1888–1949

Lowell's elegy on his father is a rich blend of compassion, humour, sorrow and asperity. While the child bones up in his bedroom on French army generals, his father lives in a nostalgic wash of faded naval slang. The end of the poem celebrates the height of Lowell's father's career—achieved at the age of nineteen and followed by little which justified that early promise. It's hard to see quite why the quotation from Mallarmé's 'Brise Marine' should be there (*à la clarté déserte de sa lampe—by the empty brilliance of his lamp*); perhaps its very incongruity, its suggestion of young, romantic extremity, is its point.

It is in his relationship to his father that Lowell's uneasy affair with tradition and the past becomes most poignant. He habitually presents New England as a dream that has faded and gone sour. Here his own father seems to enact the dissolution of that tradition. Commander Lowell's weakness and inopportune boyishness, careless and high-spending, becomes part of a larger process of decay. The holiday clothes and holiday manners of the summer vacationers at Mattapoisett, a small resort just north of New Bedford in Massachusetts, are what New England has come to: the provincial silly outgrowth of a great and dignified past.

Page 66   'Sailing Home From Rapallo'

Again the colours of black and yellow—brought together in his mother's ornate coffin—as Lowell crosses from Italy to New England with her body. Yellow here is the colour of the Mediterranean spring, while New Hampshire is still locked in a black winter. But it is the black severity of the Dunbarton graveyard, the resting place of a whole New England tradition, which jars so incongruously against the entirely twentieth-century messiness of his parents' lives, and the manner of their deaths. The *panetone* of the last line is Italian hot bread, wrapped in tinfoil to keep it warm at the table; here tinfoil encases his mother's corpse to insulate it from the Mediterranean heat. The misspelling of the family name underlines the way in which the family and what it stands for in New England history have sunk into an inglorious anonymity.

Page 67   *'Waking in the Blue'*

This poem, along with 'Home After Three Months Away', was the source for a fashion amongst American poets of the 1960s; its frank treatment of Lowell's experience in a mental hospital was used as a model for a number of dramatised 'confessions' of psychiatric illness. 'Confessional verse' was to become a label for an unbuttoned style of reminiscence practised by Lowell's imitators. That said, it is important to emphasize the continuity which this poem maintains with the themes of Lowell's earlier work. Its setting ('Bowditch Hall at McLean's', which sounds—deliberately—collegiate, is, in fact, the ward of a private hospital in Belmont, Massachusetts) is really incidental; a variant of the prisons, graveyards and holiday beaches which Lowell identifies as the theatres in which the continuous tragicomedy of New England is being played out.

The 'B.U. sophomore' is a student from Boston University, where Lowell was teaching at the time, and I. A. Richards, the co-author of *The Meaning of Meaning*, was and is an old friend of Lowell's and a Harvard professor. Note the whaling image, echoing *Moby Dick*, in line 9; the precipitous edge of knowledge, the delirious hunger of Captain Ahab for the blood of the white whale, is one of Lowell's constant preoccupations. In his earlier poems it was associated with sin (as it was for Melville); here it is linked with mania—the terrible clarity of madness. 'Stanley' and 'Bobby', both one-time Harvard stars ('Porcellian' is the name of an exclusive Harvard club), are the pathetic relics of yet another New England tradition. Lowell's epitaph on them—'These victorious figures of bravado ossified young'—might stand as an epitaph on all the major characters in *Life Studies*, their unfulfilled promise, their failure to live up to the history they have inherited. Lowell has said that his experience in mental hospitals taught him a degree of humility; in this poem we see him participating in the failure of New England with a sympathy that is humble, compassionate, and profound. The final stanza in the poem is for me one of the most moving passages in all his work.

Page 70   *'Memories of West Street and Lepke'*

From the 1950s, and the slovenly freedom of university teaching,

Lowell returns to his prison term in 1943–4. Note the ironic juxta-position of the garbage man's symbols of affluence and the glorious Lowellian hyperbole of his description of his daughter Harriet. The image of her as a rising sun in her 'flame-flamingo infants' wear' shines out over the rest of the poem: Harriet's baby future is set against Lowell's own past. His fellow prisoners, famous in their way as the great Boston families in his other poems, have an odd, stiff dignity. The notorious gang-murderer Czar Lepke, with his trappings of Catholicism and patriotism, turns into the shambling *alter ego* of the poet himself.

Page 72   *'Man and Wife'*
Miltown is a proprietary tranquillizer. It is also a pun, for Lowell here echoes Milton's opening lines in *Paradise Lost*, Book 2:

> High on a throne of a royal state, which far
> Outshone the wealth of Ormus and of Ind,
> Or where the gorgeous East with richest hand
> Showers on her kings barbaric pearl and gold,
> Satan exalted sat . . .

In Lowell's poem, this splendid throne has changed into the marital bed of his, twelve-year-old marriage, as Lowell stands again on the edge of mania. The 'Rahvs' whom he outdrank in Greenwich Village are, presumably, the American critic Philip Rahv and his wife; an example of Lowell's often maddening habit of making entirely private references public in his verse.

Page 74   *'Skunk Hour'*
Lowell has said that this poem was inspired by Elizabeth Bishop's 'The Armadillo'. It is set in Castine, Maine, where Lowell and his family had a summer home. The 'hermit heiress', the departed 'summer millionaire' (L. L. Bean is a well-known Maine mail-order firm), and the 'fairy decorator' are all figures of abandonment and isolation. The poet himself, a lone voyeur of the teenage 'love-cars', takes on the desolation of this corrupted graveyard of other people's hopes. Note the way in which the metrical poise of the fifth and sixth stanzas is broken in their final lines, as Lowell arrives at a style of painfully direct statement.

Animals (see, for instance, 'Words for a Guinea Pig') have a special place in Lowell's imaginative world. His skunks and guinea-pigs, like his fish, are a universe apart from his people. They have a self-contained, instinctive grace that the human beings in Lowell's poetry are always doomed to fall short of. Their unreflective, unselfconscious stupidity is their salvation. In 'Skunk Hour' there is a reserved lightening of tone in the poem as the skunks take over Castine for the night; their gravely secure domestic life, as they blindly pass the church in search of the garbage cans, is to be both loved and envied.

Page 79   *'Water'*

Both this poem and 'The Old Flame' are closely related to 'Skunk Hour'. In 'Water' Lowell works with an unprecedentedly simple style of plain statement and bare simile. It borrows its rhythm from the slap of the waves on the rock, and its mermaid, fish and gulls are, like the skunks, augurs of a yearned for yet unattainable instinctive and elemental life. The flatness of the final line of the poem, 'the water was too cold for us', points up the impossibility of the dreams which the poem encloses. Just as the rock turns darker and darker in the memory, so the life of mermaids and returning souls has gone black, cold, rotting. As the first poem in a collection (*For the Union Dead*) which Lowell has said was written in a state of depression, the simple sombriety of 'Water' sets a tone which later poems pick up and elaborate.

Page 80   *'The Old Flame'*

This poem keeps up a delicate play between the 'old flame', Lowell's wife, and the 'Old Glory', the national flag whose colours of red, white, and blue are repeated in the final stanza when the snow-plough goes by. The summer cottage has been refurbished by new tenants in a vulgarly patriotic style, as if the American Dream itself could be renewed with flags and colonial-antique bric-à-brac. Lowell catches that crude belief in the possibility of the new frontier with tender irony. Is the 'old flame' also the continuing flicker of optimism in the American character? By the eighth stanza, has Lowell's wife been transmuted into the spirit of an ancient America, still calling fitfully to a degenerated modern world? And is her 'ghostly/ imaginary lover' the figure of Death, and whose death does he augur?

Page 82   *'Fall 1961'*

An ornate antique grandfather clock provides the rhythm and much of the imagery for this poem. The rhymes and metrics are recurrent and obsessional. 'Fall 1961' takes up from where 'Mr Edwards and

171

the Spider' left off; time, in the ticking of the clock, and the passing of summer through autumn, is measured again against the hapless, timeless life of spiders and minnows. Does Lowell mean to identify the swinging of the pendulum with the metrical *tick-tock* of metre? Is his 'one point of rest' actually the writing of the poem, the ordering of time in the metrical patterns of verse?

Page 84   '*Eye and Tooth*'

A poem about exhausted, perpetually aggravated vision, this, like 'Fall 1961', seems to be concerned with the pain and the release of writing poetry. Lowell treats his cut cornea as if it had been caused by the pressure of remembered images from his childhood. To go on living is to go on seeing, and there is in this poem no point of rest: 'Even new life is fuel'. Is the sharp-shinned hawk clasping the abstract imperial sky a picture of the American eagle? Its grim Old Testament message might stand as an epigraph to many of Lowell's more recent poems. His own verse makes art live off pain and death—takes, as it were, an eye for an eye and a tooth for a tooth.

Page 85   '*Law*'

One law for civic man, another for the imagination. As a child, Lowell breaks the law by fishing in forbidden reservoirs out of season. 'Bass-plugging' is fishing for the freshwater bass with an imitation dead-fish made out of coloured wood and metal. Yet breaking the law as a citizen leads him into another broken law: in the unlikely landscape of Massachusetts a vision opens up of a courtly, medieval Europe. The boundary between reality and dream is fine; the circumscription of law and convention is easily erased. In Lowell's poem, past and present, America and Europe, commingle, bought into a fluid state by that initial act of trespass.

Page 86   '*The Public Garden*'

A Boston civic park in autumn is seen as an arid, burned-out shadow of the Garden of Eden before the Fall. Here the only use for the great languages of the past is to make Latin labels for the trees. The only creatures still engaged on a quest are the rootling mallards. The brilliantly particularized landscape of the poem has the detailed immediacy of a Dutch painting, but it turns to metaphor at the word 'Eden': the public garden is nothing less than the fallen world.

Page 87   *'Returning'*

Another frizzled landscape, with memories of greener times. The only green thing in the town now is the traffic-light. By the fourth stanza, the speaker of the poem seems to be Adam: is the deadness of the town a direct result of the birth and first quenching of his lust? The poem has the generalized, abstracted tone of an allegorical statement, but I find its effect tantalizing, puzzling and oblique.

Page 88   *'The Drinker'*

Another Adamic figure, trapped and festering in the junk of urban life. Lowell's malodorous technological imagery—the harpoon in the whale's belly, the 'galvanized bucket', the 'iron lung' of the central-heating system—prevails over the human in this poem, and, in the penultimate stanza, takes on a sinister, decaying life of its own. Is the man killing time, or is time killing him? Notice how, in the final lines, the magical splash of spring, and the promise of a beauty beyond the drinker's window, are themselves occasioned by a technological material—the yellow PVC of the policemen's oilskins. Here, as in other poems written during the early 1960s, Lowell's style is self-consciously surrealist; objects are endowed with the same vivid and unlikely activity that they display in the work of painters like Magritte and Dali.

Page 90   *'Tenth Muse'*

Compare this poem with 'Law', p. *85*, for its exploration of the corruptible frailty of human laws and conventions. The laws of Moses are engraved on stones 'we cannot bear or break', and Sloth, the tenth muse, inspires the poet with boredom and resignation before the insoluble problems of human conduct. The poem is light in texture, memorable for the occasional brilliance of its images (the 'malignant surf of unopened letters') and the bravado of its epigrams ('even God was born/ too late to trust the old religion'). The verse is freer, the wit more generalized and public, than in most of Lowell's earlier work. This poem foreshadows the later, oracular, epigrammatic style of *Notebook*.

Page 91   *'July in Washington'*

Washington D.C. is the hub of American political power; and in Lowell's poem the power-launches doodling on the Potomac River seem to be standing in for the planes and boats and delegations which go from Washington to Vietnam and the other 'sore spots of the earth'. As in 'Inauguration Day: January 1953', p. *55*, politicians are represented by their immobile statues, effigies of power without names, personalities or feelings. 'The Elect', the old American Calvinist doctrine of a community of saints existing by divine grace, have turned into 'the elected'—mere puppets of the ballot-box. Lowell's own politics, as they show up in his poems, are not so much conservative as High Tory: he treats the machinery of government with aristocratic disdain—as an enervating, vulgarizing force that is more likely to sap human life than support it. The farther shore of the last three couplets of the poem hints at an Edenic world beyond politics; a dream of an untrammeled and mysterious freedom. Yet, very delicately, Lowell reminds us why we need politics, why that mausoleum of Washington is inevitable and necessary. What will drag us back to Washington is 'the slightest repugnance of our bodies/ we no longer control . . .'. The free man on the farther shore returns to the world of edicts and laws motivated by that negative principle of distaste for uncontrolled liberation. Man, in Lowell's work, is always bad at being free, and this conviction saturates all his political writing.

Page 92   *'Soft Wood'*

This, like 'Fourth of July in Maine', p. *104*, is a summer letter to Lowell's cousin, written from and about the house in Maine which she has lent him and his family. The white-painted, wood-shingled houses of New England belong to a more illustrious past, possessions that have outlasted their possessors; 'Shed skin will never fit another wearer.' The seals, the wood and the weather go on, while people grow old and die. As so often in his work, Lowell worries at this seemingly unoriginal insight until it becomes entirely his own: in 'Soft Wood' he lives in Maine, symbol of New England tradition, like a trespasser, guilty, consumed by his sense of his own mortality. The appalling clarity and truth of the last line floods back over the whole of the rest of the poem. Like the drug, the other constituents of the poem—the summer vacation, the absorption in New England history—simultaneously numb and alert to pain. Much of his characteristic tentativeness and obliquity at this period may be attributed to Lowell's wary knowledge of the double-edgedness of experience, so dazzlingly condensed in this last line.

Page 93   *'The Flaw'*

Like 'Eye and Tooth', p. *84*, and 'Flaw (Flying to Chicago)', p. *140*, this poem elaborates, in the style of a metaphysical conceit, the image of the hairline cut on the cornea of Lowell's eye. His vision of the external world is murky, yet the flaw, shaped like a question mark, drives him to a startling and detailed vision of the internal world of the human spirit. In the final line, the senses are surrealistically confused: 'how will you hear my answer in the dark?'

Page 95　　　　　　　　*'For the Union Dead'*
In 1865, a hundred years before the publication of this poem, Lowell's ancestor James Russell Lowell recited an Ode to the Union dead at the Harvard Commemoration ceremony. J. R. Lowell's poem is slight and fulsome:

> We sit here in the Promised Land
> That flows with Freedom's honey and milk;
> But 'twas they won it, sword in hand,
> Making the nettle danger soft as silk.
> We welcome back our bravest and our best;—
> Ah me! not all! some come not with the rest . . .

In 1928, Allen Tate, Lowell's teacher and mentor, published his richly rhetorical 'Ode to the Confederate Dead'. 'For the Union Dead' is, at one level, administered as a corrective to both the piety and the rhetoric of its predecessors. It is a proud, savage, ultimately despairing appraisal of the state of New England one hundred years after the Civil War. The grand Latin inscription on the bronze memorial to Colonel Shaw's infantry—'They gave up everything to serve the Republic'—is belied by a modern Boston of underground car-parks and TV. Automobiles have replaced the fish of the aquarium; a patent safe—symbol of rude cash—is shown in an advertisement withstanding the blast of a nuclear bomb. The severe, puritan idealism of Colonel Shaw is tragically misplaced in the centre of this vulgarized twentieth-century city. Shaw is, perhaps, an odd hero for Lowell; a soldier, a commander of a regiment of blacks. Yet in the ninth stanza, Lowell might be writing about himself; his own style in this poem, solemn, observant, restrained, is full of Shaw's 'angry wrenlike vigilance', wincing at pleasure and suffocating for privacy.

The 'savage servility' which 'slides by on grease' is the most forceful image Lowell has ever found to embody the version of the modern world which he sees as terrible and threatening. It is everything that the best in American history has stood against; it runs counter to the proud ideals of both the Puritans and the cause of the Union forces in the Civil War. Notice the wayward black irony in the fifth stanza where the orange girders of the modern vandals are 'Puritan-pumpkin colored'—their colour is the only thing that is remotely puritan about them. What is 'the blessed break' which Shaw—and Lowell—awaits? And what is the relationship between the bubble on which Shaw rides and the bubbles that drifted from the mouths of the Aquarium fish in Lowell's childhood? The poem has an intricate, submerged frame of interrelated images, all drawn from the 'dark downward and vegetating kingdom/ of the fish and reptile' which Lowell writes of in the third stanza. Is this the kingdom into which twentieth-century man is sinking fast?

Page 101   '*Waking Early Sunday Morning*'

Lowell's most celebrated political poem. In *Armies of the Night* Norman Mailer brilliantly describes how Lowell read this poem to an audience of war demonstrators in Washington on the eve of the Pentagon march in October 1967. 'Waking Early Sunday Morning' began, so Lowell says, with the shape and rhythm of Marvell's eight-line stanza humming in his head all summer. He has used the same stanza form for 'Fourth of July in Maine' and 'Near the Ocean', and, clearly, feels a strong affinity with Marvell, the public poet of the seventeenth century and author of the most famous political poem in the language, the 'Horatian Ode on Cromwell's Return from Ireland'. Lowell's own public poetry is in some ways astonishingly similar to Marvell's: it hunts, like Marvell's, for the private men behind the public faces; it shares the same equivocal obsession with heroes and heroic action. It comes to the same tortured and ambiguous conclusions about the final virtue of privacy. Marvell's famous, double-edged tribute to Cromwell:

> Who, from his private Gardens, where
> He liv'd reserved and austere,
>   As if his highest plot
>   To plant the Bergamot,
> Could by industrious valour climbe
> To ruin the great Work of Time,
>   And cast the Kingdom old
>   Into another mold.

—is here echoed in Lowell's portrait of the American president, 'swimming nude, unbuttoned, sick/ of his ghost-written rhetoric!'

The whole poem is finely balanced on a fulcrum: on one side, the private weekend freedom of the poet with his vision of a liberated nature; and on the other, a public world in misery and chains, a world of madness, war, pogroms and political assassinations. 'Waking Early Sunday Morning' is a profound self-examination: Lowell's own freedom to feel and think—the freedom, indeed, to write the poem—is harshly and ironically contrasted with the global unfreedom of our century. His 'unpolluted joy' turns, in the space of a line, to 'the criminal leisure of a boy'. In the penultimate stanza, note how Lowell uses the traditional pastoral image of the reaper: what is being reaped is human life in a war of bombs and napalm. And in the last line, the sublime—the ultimate aesthetic harmony to which all art was supposed to aspire—is represented by a lifeless, self-murdered cosmos. Such radical and savage ironies are, perhaps, the necessary fate of the twentieth-century political poet to whom Marvell's equivocal answers have become unavailable.

Page 104   *'Fourth of July in Maine'*
Compare with 'Soft Wood', p. *92*; this poem is also closely related to both 'For the Union Dead' and 'Waking Early Sunday Morning'. On the holiday anniversary of American Independence, Lowell broods over the fate of American history, that 'dark design/ spun by God and Cotton Mather'. Mather (1663–1728) was a puritan divine who watched jealously over the health of New England in the period of its first political and spiritual self-appraisal. The dream of a golden state—'bel eta dell' oro'—has faded; and the two Harriets—Lowell's elderly cousin and his daughter—embody a doubtful continuity between a dying past and a troubled future. This poem is as near to light verse as Lowell has ever come—a comic holiday epistle.

Page 109   *'Central Park'*
Central Park, New York, is a green lung of an overcrowded city by day, and a notorious haunt of hoodlums and muggers by night. Lowell's poem follows the transition from day to night, and Central Park, 'this dying crust', is ambiguously identified with the world itself, passing from the desperate ecstasies of the lovers, through the caged lion and lost kitten, to the image of the Pharaohs, hideously mummified amongst the trophies of their earthly riches. Lowell has said that he wrote 'Central Park' at a time when he was in analysis, and had to cross the park each afternoon to visit

his analyst. Its tone of brooding retrospection is, perhaps, connected with the rehearsal of personal history made by someone undergoing psychotherapy. From the centre of the richest and possibly most violent city in the history of the world, Lowell contemplates a civilization trapped by its own errors: only the paper kite, symbol of the frailest human aspirations to transcendence, manages to rise through the smog that lies over this doomed patch of ground.

Page 111   *'Near the Ocean'*

I find this Lowell's most difficult poem, full of phantasmagoric connections; it seems to work with the partial logic of a nightmare. Is the theatrical setting of the opening lines a stage for a Greek tragedy, or a modern movie-house? The 'hero' seems to be Perseus, raising the head of the dead Medusa, one of the Gorgons, who was pregnant by the god Neptune. (The gouts of blood turned into snakes and infested the continent of Africa with reptiles.) Yet Medusa is also a more generalized figure of Woman; she turns into Clytemnestra, mother of Orestes, and later into Eve. As in 'Beyond the Alps', p. *53*, there is a doomed historical continuity: the third stanza appears to reach back to Troy and forward to the contemporary Arab-Israeli conflict, in its catalogue of 'abortions and mistakes' that make up the 'Near Eastern dreck'. The poem then shifts to New England, to a despoiled Eden and an exhausted marriage. The ocean, symbol, simultaneously, of recurrence, permanence and immediacy, both consoles and incites to despair. Is the 'Monster' in the final couplet Woman?—Eve and Medusa, temptress, serpent, muse? Try reading the poem as a sequence of discontinuous scenes, each one an enactment of Man's relations with Woman.

Page 117   *Poems from* Notebook

The sonnets printed here were originally published in Lowell's *Notebook* (1970). He was dissatisfied with the looseness and discontinuity (in some quarters this had been the book's most highly praised feature) of that collection, and in 1973 he rewrote and rearranged the poems to form two separate books, *History* and *For Lizzie and Harriet*. It is these later versions of the poems that are published in this selection. However, all three of the books, and *The Dolphin* too, are not so much 'collections' as long complete poems, and selecting from them is a difficult and invidious task. The individual sonnets take fire from the continuing obsessions and themes of each book; alone, they burn less brightly. The reader is advised to try reading the selection from *Notebook* as if it was part of a single poem before he returns in detail to the line-by-line workings of each sonnet. My own annotations of the *Notebook* poems follows the same pattern.

Notebook, as it originally appeared, was Lowell's mammoth poem-novel. Its hero is the poet himself, and the book is an elaborate projection of his personal, social and intellectual life. It interweaves history, autobiography and fiction and is a record of a man living in the second half of the twentieth century armed with a passionate sensibility, a wide and deep reading in the literature of the past, and a severe and critical self-knowledge. In *Notebook* ('First Love', p. *120*) Lowell refers to Flaubert as 'the supreme artist' and this invocation has a special significance for the pattern of the whole poem. Flaubert took the vulgarity and muddle of nineteenth-century France and turned them into a perfectly formed, ironically phrased fiction. In the figure of Frederic Moreau in *The Sentimental Education*, Flaubert half-mockingly, half-heroically, externalised himself and his passage through the bourgeois-literary world of France. So Lowell in *Notebook* treats himself, his love affairs and marriage, his engagement in literary and political life, with a slight yet eloquent Flaubertian exaggeration. The 'I' of the poem is a hyperbolic first person, a being who has attained the mythic proportions of fiction while at the same time keeping one foot at least firmly in the world of fact. As a result there is, throughout the poem, an undertone of heroic comedy; we respond to its hero, as we respond to Frederic Moreau, with a delicate mixture of sympathy and detachment.

Lowell's sonnets, in a typically Flaubertian gesture, are often adaptations of letters and conversations. They take the language of the outside world, its talk and writing, and admit it to the cramped sanctum of the form of the sonnet. Lowell delights in that tension—between form and material—and the rub of everyday language against the hard edge of the poetic line is one of the major preoccupations of *Notebook*. In 'Clytemnestra', p. *121*, much of the original material may be found in his autobiographical prose sketch, '91 Revere Street' (published in the collection *Life Studies*):

> Mother hated the Navy, hated naval society, naval pay, and the trip-hammer rote of settling and unsettling a house every other year when Father was transferred to a new station or ship. She had been married nine or ten years and still suspected that her husband was savourless, unmasterful, merely considerate. . . . Fully conscious of her uniqueness and normality she basked in

the refreshing stimulation of dreams in which she imagined Father as suitably sublimed. She used to describe such a sublime man to me over tea and English muffins. . . .

Similarly in 'Publication Day', p. *140*, Lowell makes a sonnet out of a letter he receives from a woman who writes unpublished poems. Her style, awkward, naïve, a little affected, brushes against his own, and it is the tension between the two that the poem happens. In 'Growth', p. *142*, we hear Lowell's daughter Harriet coming into the poem in her own words; in 'Women, Children, Babies, Cows, Cats', p. *141*, Lowell turns the horrifying testimony of a soldier at the My Lai massacre into a poem; and in 'West Side Sabbath', p *136*, Lowell brilliantly transforms an icy breakfast table conversation between husband and wife into a sonnet.

Such intrusions of raw, relatively unadjusted life, are part of a larger, central theme of the poem as a whole. There is a constant, often anguished investigation of the paradox by which the poet is doomed to turn the untidy stuff of life into the formal perfection of art. In *Notebook* Lowell has submitted his entire life to the demands of artistic form—has turned his own passion and pain into the pre-served, dead eloquence of the sonnet sequence. Yet it is only through his work that the poet lives. In 'Reading Myself', p. *138*, Lowell sees himself as a bee making a mausoleum of honey and wax that awaits only the bear to 'desecrate' it; in 'Onion Skin', p. *122*, he develops an elaborate life-in-death conceit around his typing paper. Trees have to be killed and cut down to make paper; Lowell needs paper to live in his poem; and out of these simple facts he springs a glittering, paradoxical final couplet:

> as if Fortuna bled in the white wood,
> and felt the bloody gash that brought me life.

So, too, in 'New Year's Eve 1968', the sunset on the Hudson River, symbol of new life and the new year, is rendered by a black, dead line of type:

> bright sky, bright sky, carbon scarred with ciphers.

But the centre of *Notebook*, like the centre of most novels, lies in the intense, brilliantly dramatized, lives of its characters. The 'Charles River' sequence, p. *123*, shows Lowell at his most personal, most accessible—a poet writing with a novelist's passion for the human incident and detail. It is a zigzagging narrative: it starts in middle-age and marriage on the banks of the Charles River as it flows through Cambridge, Massachusetts past the buildings of the university of Harvard. In the second sonnet in the sequence Lowell is a child, trailed by the figure of Woman (another Eve/Medusa/Clytemnestra?) as he follows his male ski-instructor. By the third sonnet, Woman was solidified into Anne Dick and Lowell's student love affair which triggered the violent row with his father. His writing here is as compressed and ardent as anything in his work. But the fourth sonnet, in which Lowell himself assumes the age of the father he knocked down thirty years before, brings us back into the present as it is shaped by events in the past. Making rapid associative leaps from period to period, character to character, Lowell still maintains the thread of continuous narrative. In the fifth sonnet, his parents die, first symbolically at the hand of their son, then actually, in 1950 and 1954. In the sixth sonnet, he returns to Anne Dick, echoing Donne:

> I wonder by my troth, what thou and I
> Did, till we lov'd? were we not weaned till then?

Lowell's rephrasing of these lines in 'Longer ago than I had lived till then' seems subliminal, suggestively inexact, but the irony is savage. In the unconscious sleep of the lovers before they had met one another there happened, not the pastoral, drowsy pleasures of Donne's 'Good Morrow', but the most bloody war in history, now no more than a casual memory. The 'hideous concrete dome' of the Massachusetts Institute of Technology is the only temple in the lovers' landscape; and the forgiving figure of Christ at the end of the sonnet becomes, paradoxically, a symbol of the very forces which have loosed these ills upon the world. Lowell's Christ has been misused, invoked in the name of war and industry and murder. In the seventh and eighth sonnets, Cambridge turns into a Stygean underworld, the Charles its River Styx; technology has taken over from the human, car headlights have replaced the stars. These are 'wrong times, an evil dispensation', and the people, 'unhappy and awake' seem to be souls in Purgatory, reliving the sins of their past.

The intricate tessellation of these themes, with each sonnet deepening and expanding the cumulative burden of the poems before it, may be taken as a model, in miniature, of the way in which *Notebook* works at large. The individual poems are complete in themselves, yet they are also like paragraphs in a novel. Here, more than anywhere else in his work, we can come to terms with the full, eccentric force of Lowell's imagination, zigzagging and leap-frogging through history, autobiography, literature and myth. His connections and associations are logically arbitrary, but imaginatively profound; and the speed with which they are made, dropped, taken up again, is astonishing.

The remaining notes to the *Notebook* poems take up some of the more difficult references made in individual sonnets, and they follow the order in which the poems are printed in this selection.

Page 117   '*Harriet*'
In an 'Afterthought', published in the 1970 edition of *Notebook*, Lowell wrote:

> My opening lines are as hermetic as any in the book. The 'fractions' mean that my daughter, born in January, is each July, a precision important to a child, something and a half years old. The 'Seaslug, etc.' are her declining conceptions of God.

The 'Harriet' poems were written a few months after the first production of Lowell's version of *Prometheus Bound*, and Lowell echoes Prometheus at the end of the first sonnet. In his play he made Prometheus say:

> Around some bend, under some moving stone, behind some thought, if it were ever the right thought, I will find my key. No, not just another of Nature's million petty clues, but a key, *my key*, *the* key, the one that must be there, because it can't be there—a face still friendly to chaos.

In the second sonnet, the 'Arabs on a screen' were to be seen during the six-day war in June 1967 between Israel and Egypt. Juliet, in *Romeo and Juliet*, referred to in the fourth sonnet, was supposed to have been aged fourteen, but the beginnings of puberty have made Harriet, at ten, already 'half-Juliet'.

Page 122   '*The March*'
The peace march on the Pentagon took place on 21st October 1967. Lowell's part in it has been described by Norman Mailer in *The Armies of the Night*.

Page 130   '*Die Forelle*'
This poem is Lowell's response to Schubert's *The Trout*.

While living in Italy in the 1939–45 war, Ezra Pound made a number of pro-fascist radio broadcasts. When the war ended, he was indicted in the United States, and detained in Saint Elizabeth's Hospital for the Criminally Insane, where Lowell visited him and was one of many American writers who campaigned for Pound's release. 'Possum's *hommage* to Milton' was Eliot's postwar reconsideration of Milton, a poet whom, in 1936, he had attacked in a famous essay in *Essays and Studies*.

In 'Exorcism 2.' Lowell writes:

> My words are English, but the plot is hexed:
> one man, two women, the common novel plot.

Notebook deals with Lowell's second marriage and with the bleak prospect of America under Nixon, a cheapened, devalued country. *The Dolphin* opens with Lowell in England; a new life, a new marriage. The dolphin herself, part fish, part mermaid, part woman, moves through the new book, always almost out of reach. She stands, more unequivocally than any other of Lowell's major symbols, for the possibility of a renewed life of peace, grace and charity. The book moves to a climax around the birth of Lowell's first son, Robert Sheridan Lowell, born in 1971; and the sonnet which bears his name closes with the announcement of a miracle—'we have escaped our death-struggle with our lives'.

Lowell's earlier poems are possessed by the past; *The Dolphin* is his first work in celebration of the present and future, and it is coloured, even at its darkest moments of fear and mental disturbance, by a continuous deep joy. The individual sonnets are clearer, more nearly lyrical, more confidently personal, than any poems he has written before. Its landscape of London and Kent is as freshly lit as the landscape of an Italian renaissance painting; we watch Lowell exploring England with the openness of vision of the original colonists of his own New England—he is alert to its life without being burdened by its history. The Englishness of *The Dolphin* is partly accidental, a product of Lowell's biography; but it is also symbolic. Lowell, following in the footsteps of Hawthorne, James, Henry Adams and T. S. Eliot, is an American discovering England, reversing the westward journey of his ancestors. His earlier poems present New England as a fallen Eden; Kent and

London come perhaps a little closer to the innocence of the Garden than the desolated wasteland of modern America.

But the dolphin is more than a woman and a country; it is an ideal of poetic form. As a lover and an immigrant, Lowell in *The Dolphin* is in the thrall of a new wife and a new landscape; as a writer, he is in the thrall of form and plot, a creature of his own imaginative artifice. We see him living out the story he is writing, an actor in the grip of a text. Even more intensely than in *Notebook*, the life and the book are inseparably married; he lives to write and writes to live. The poem itself is not a record of that life but its most profound and vivid enactment. Tender, hopeful and understanding, the poet, like a mariner following the wake of a mythical dolphin, moves into an uncharted future.

Page 147   *'Fishnet'*
This is close in tone to the poems-about-poems in *Notebook*; here Lowell seems to be echoing Yeats's images of artifice in 'Byzantium':

> Once out of nature I shall never take
> My bodily form from any natural thing,
> But such a form as Grecian goldsmiths make
> Of hammered gold and gold enamelling
> To keep a drowsy emperor awake;
> Or set upon a golden bough to sing
> To lords and ladies of Byzantium
> Of what is past, or passing, or to come.

Lowell's 'fishnet of tarred rope' is his poetic work; the fish that will be eaten are the life from which his poems spring. The 'wandering silences and bright trouvailles' of the 'you' in the opening lines might equally well belong to a woman or a poem.

Page 148   *'Fall Weekend at* Milgate'
Milgate is the name of the country house in Kent where Lowell lives with his family. Compare the wasps of this poem with the bear and the bee in 'Reading Myself', p. 138.

Page 149   The *'Mermaid'* poems
These poems are addressed both by a real man to a real woman and by a mythical mariner to a mermaid and a dolphin.

Page 151   *'Flounder'*

A brilliantly elaborated metaphysical conceit, punning 'sole' with 'soul'. The sole which Lowell consumes alone in a London restaurant is as far from the dolphin as a fish can go, an innocent, pitiable parasite. Notice how delicately Lowell turns London into an undersea world, an ocean as deep as the one where soles and dolphins swim.

Page 151–2   *'Exorcism'* and *'Plotted'*

Three related images: a movie screen, a novel, and a theatre. As in 'Near the Ocean', p. *111*, Lowell uses the metaphor of public performance much as Marvell employed it in the 'Horatian Ode':

> . . . That thence the *Royal Actor* born
> The *Tragick Scaffold* might adorn:
> While round the Armed Bands
> Did clap their bloody hands.
> *He* nothing common did or mean
> Upon that memorable scene . . .

Private life turns into a public spectacle, played out in the theatre of the world. The 'I' of Lowell's poem is both private man and tragic actor, and the poem itself is the projector by which the one is transmuted into the other. In 'Plotted' he says, 'I execute my written plot', and the pun is savage. In writing he at once creates life—*executes* the book as a skilled artist—and destroys it, *executing* it like a hangman. He is both author and victim of his own poetic form and conventions, 'stuck' with that 'common novel plot' which always threatens to turn into melodrama and revenge tragedy. The consequences are as important for his life as they are for his book.

Page 152   *'Artist's Model'*

The strain of the theatre and the plot result in the private human confusion of the last line, 'I come on walking off-stage backwards'.

Page 153   *'Mermaid Emerging'*

A deeply ambiguated poem. Degas's snub-nosed dancer who enchants lovers of art but discerns none is, like the dolphin, both a real woman and a figure of artifice—on two levels, for she is both herself an artist and a configuration of paint made by Degas, another artist. The speaking voice in the second half of the poem talks for both the dolphin as woman and the dolphin as elusive poetic form.

Page 154   '*Late Summer at* Milgate'

Lowell and the country house itself speak together in this poem. The old house is being rehabilitated, and Lowell too. 'My varnish complaining, *I will never die*' is the house, being changed and renewed with each new tenant, symbol at once of permanence and dilapidation. But the poem is littered with hints of mortality and infidelity—gravestones and fallen apples from Eden. 'The breath of spirits' exuded by the apples is double edged: simultaneously the whisky-smell of bruised and rotten fruit, and the promise of life . . . and knowledge.

Page 155   '*Careless Night*'

The birth of his own son and the birth of Christ are gently intermingled. The moonlit Kentish landscape blends into Bethlehem. But there are darker ironies. The 'drifter' shepherds and their 'breezy' pipe are more suggestive of hippies with penny-whistles than of the shepherds who attended Christ's birth; the crying child and the fears of death hinted at in the last line swing the poem firmly back to a mortal, twentieth-century world.

Page 156   '*Lost Fish*'

There are four fish in the poem. One was glimpsed, a figure of incomprehensible power, when the poet was seven. The second was lost, and it blends into a third, Lowell's second wife, Elizabeth Hardwick. The fourth fish, not lost, is, of course, the dolphin.

Page 158   '*Dolphin*'

This is Lowell's most personal and powerful statement about his life and work. It commands more attention than exegesis.

For Further Reading

London Boyers (*editor*), *Robert Lowell: a Portrait of the Artist in his Time*, New York, 1970, Lewis.

Philip Cooper, *The Autobiographical Myth of Robert Lowell*, Chapel Hill, 1970, University of North Carolina Press.

Patrick Cosgrave, *The Public Poetry of Robert Lowell*, London, 1970, Gollancz.

Jerome Mazzaro, *The Poetic Themes of Robert Lowell*, Ann Arbor, 1965.

Gabriel Pearson, 'Robert Lowell', *The Review*, No. 20, March 1969.

Hugh B. Staples, *Robert Lowell: the First Twenty Years*, London, 1962, Faber.

Interviews

A. Alvarez, 'Robert Lowell in Conversation with A. Alvarez', *The Review*, No. 8, August 1963.

Ian Hamilton, 'A Conversation with Robert Lowell', *The Review*, No. 26, Summer 1971.

Frederick Seidel, 'Robert Lowell: An Interview', *Writers at Work: The Paris Review Interviews, Second Series*, reprinted in *Modern Poets on Modern Poetry*, ed. by James Scully, London, 1966, Fontana.

Index of First Lines